Patanjali and Yoga

MIRCEA ELIADE

Translated by Charles Lam Markmann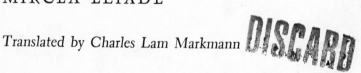

SCHOCKEN BOOKS · NEW YORK

6/01

First published by SCHOCKEN BOOKS 1975

French Edition Copyright © 1962 by Editions du Seuil

Translation Copyright © 1969 by Funk & Wagnalls

Library of Congress Cataloging in Publication Data

Eliade, Mircea, 1907-
 . . . Patanjali and Yoga.
Viι·ı 216 p. : ill.
    Translation of Patañjali et le Yoga.
    Reprint of the ed. published by Funk & Wagnalls, New York.
    Bibliography: p.
    1. Patañjali. 2. Yoga. I. Title.
[B132.Y6E493 1975]   181'.452   75-10785

Manufactured in The United States of America

Contents

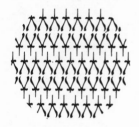

Acknowledgments

PAGE 91: M: *The Gospel of Ramakrishna*, Ramakrishna-Vivekananda Center, New York.

PAGES 191 and 198 and cover: Alain Daniélou: *Yoga, méthode de réintégration*, Éditions de l'Arche.

PAGES 64, 66, 67, 70, 73, 81, 188: Louis Frédéric: *Yoga asanas*, Oliven.

PAGES 87 and 165: Louis Frédéric: *l'Inde. Ses temples. Ses sculptures*, Arts et métiers graphiques.

INSIDE FRONT COVER: *India in the Time of Patanjali.*

PAGES 104 and 139: Archives photographiques.

PAGES 99, 109, 132, 172, 184: Publicité Roland Bardet (Éditions du Seuil).

PAGES 12, 94, 204: Bibliothèque Nationale (Éditions du Seuil).

PAGE 78: Vatican Library.

PAGES 25 and 192: Bulloz.

PAGES 64, 66, 67, 70, 73, 81, 87, 164, 188: Louis Frédéric/Rapho.

PAGES 8, 55, 80, 113, 156: Giraudon.

PAGES 4, 48, 102, 165: Musée Guimet (Éditions du Seuil).

PAGES 22, 23, 28, 37, 39, 60, 112, 118, 120, 122, 136, 137, 177, 186, 194: Richard Lannoy.

PAGES vii, 15, 19, 49, 97, 107, 143, 153: Ella Maillart.

PAGE 148: Museum of Fine Arts, Boston.

PAGE 6: Roger Viollet.

PAGES 169 and 182: Sharma-Weiss/Viollet.

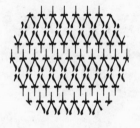

Patanjali and Yoga

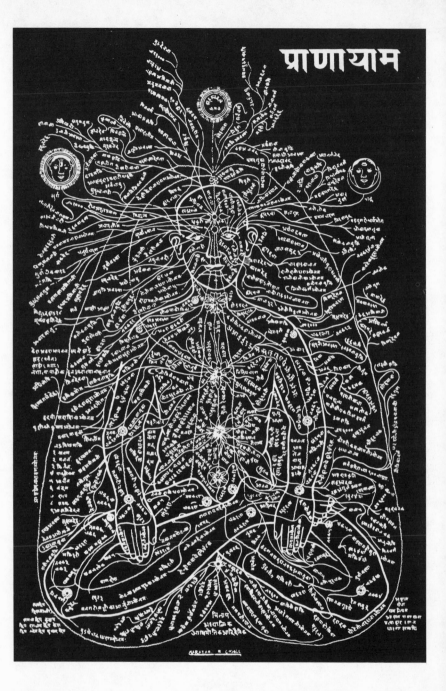

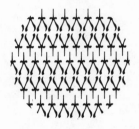

Introduction

At about the middle of the nineteenth century Dr. J. M. Honigberger astonished the scholarly world with the story of a yogi called Haridas. In the presence of Maharajah Ranjit Singh and his court in Lahore, Haridas put himself into a state of catalepsy and was buried in a garden. For forty days a strict watch was kept over the tomb. When the yogi was exhumed, he was unconscious, cold, and rigid. Hot compresses were placed on his head, he was rubbed, air was forced into his lungs in a kind of artificial respiration, and finally Haridas came back to life.

We no longer have any way of verifying this story. Such a feat, however, is not impossible. Certain yogis are capable of reducing their respiration to such a degree that they will agree

A yogi and his pupil

to be buried alive for a specified time. But the story of Haridas is significant for another reason too: His mastery of yoga in no way implied a spiritual superiority. Haridas was known, rather, as a man of loose morals. He finally fled with his wife and took refuge in the mountains. There he died and was duly buried according to the custom of the country. (See J. M. Honigberger, *Thirty-Five Years in the East*, London, 1852, pp. 125 ff.)

To Haridas yoga seems to have been primarily a fakir technique. But obviously true yoga should not be confused with the possession of a fakir's powers. Long ago Buddha warned his disciples against the possession and display of such powers: "It is precisely because I recognize the danger in the practice of fakir's powers (*iddhi:* literally, "magic marvels") that I execrate and abhor them and am ashamed of them" (Dighanikaya, I, 212 ff.). And yet Buddha himself had long practiced yoga, and Buddhism is incomprehensible without the yogic methods of concentration and meditation. Even more: No one knows of a single Indian spiritual movement that is not dependent on one of the numerous forms of yoga. For yoga is a specific dimension of the Indian mind. In the final analysis, a major part of the history of India is in fact constituted by the history of the multiple forms and aspects of what is called yogic practice.

This is readily understood if one recalls that, since the age of the Upanishads, India has been seriously concerned with only one great problem: the structure of the human condition. With a discipline unequaled elsewhere the philosophers, the contemplatives, and the ascetics have dedicated themselves to the analysis of the various "conditionings" of the human being. Let us hasten to add that they have done so not in order to achieve a precise and coherent explanation of man (as for instance in nineteenth-century Europe, when it was thought that man could be explained by his hereditary or social conditioning), but in order to know how far the conditioned areas of the human being extended and *to see whether something more existed beyond such conditioning.* It was for this reason that, long before the advent of depth psychology, the Indian

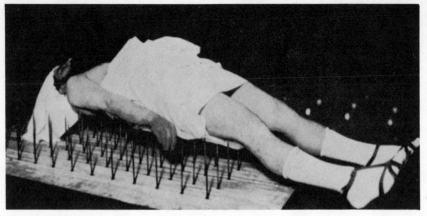

Fakir exploits

sages and ascetics were induced to explore the obscure regions of the unconscious: They had established that physical, social, cultural, and religious influences were relatively easy to delimit and, consequently, to master; the great obstacles to the ascetic and contemplative life arose out of the activity of the unconscious, the *samskaras* and the *vasanas*, the "impregnations," "residues," "latencies" that make up what depth psychology designates by the content and structures of the unconscious. But it is not this pragmatic anticipation of certain modern psychological techniques that is valuable; it is its utilization with a view to the "deconditioning" of man. For the knowledge of the systems of "conditioning" could not have its end in itself as far as India was concerned. What was important was not to know the systems but to dominate them; one labored over the content of the unconscious in order to "cauterize" it.

We shall see by what methods yoga expects to arrive at these surprising results. But it is impossible to leave out of consideration one of the greatest of India's discoveries: that of consciousness as a witness, consciousness released from its psycho-physiological structures and their temporal conditioning, the consciousness of the "delivered"—in other words, the man who has succeeded in releasing himself from temporality and therefore knows true, indescribable freedom. The conquest of this absolute freedom constitutes the goal of all the Indian philosophies and mystic techniques, but it is above all through yoga, through one of the manifold forms of yoga, that India believes that the goal has been reached.

This is the reason why certain yogis of remote antiquity deserve to be ranked among the "spiritual masters." But, since nothing is known of them, not even their names, I have included the name of Patanjali in the title of this little book. Patanjali is no less legendary than so many other figures of Hindu antiquity, but he is supposed to have written the first systematic treatise on yoga.

A yogi of the eighth century

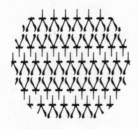

Pantanjali's Yoga

YOGA, JUNGERE, JUGUM

It is not easy to define yoga. Etymologically the word is derived from the root *yuj*, "to link together," "to bind closely," "to harness," "to bring under the yoke," and this root also is the source of the Latin *jungere* and *jugum*, the English *yoke*, etc. In general, the word *yoga* is used to distinguish every *technique of asceticism* and every *method of meditation*. Obviously these varieties of asceticism and meditation have been differently esteemed by the innumerable currents of thought and mystic movements in India. There is a "classical" yoga, expounded by Patanjali in his famous treatise, *Yoga Sutras*, and it is from this system that one must start in order to understand the position of yoga in the history of Indian thought. But, side by side with this "classical" yoga, there exist uncountable "popular" forms of yoga, which are not systematized, and there are also the non-Brahman yogas (those of the Buddhists and the Jains, for example).

Basically it is this very word, yoga, that has made this great variety of connotations possible. Although in fact, etymologically, *yuj* means "to link," it is nevertheless clear that the "bond" in which this action of linking should culminate presupposes as a condition precedent the severance of the bonds that join the spirit and the world. In other words, deliverance cannot take place unless one has first "detached oneself" from the world, unless one has begun by withdrawing from the cosmic circuit, for otherwise one would never succeed in finding oneself again or in mastering oneself. Even in its "mystic" connotation—that is, even in so far as it signifies *union*—yoga implies a prior detachment from the material, emancipation with respect to the world. The stress is placed on man's *effort* ("to bring under the yoke"), on his self-discipline, thanks to which he can achieve concentration of mind, even before he has invoked—as in the mystic varieties of yoga—the aid of the divinity. "To link together," "to bind tightly," "to bring under the yoke"—the purpose of all these actions is to *unify* the spirit, to eliminate dispersion and the automatisms that are characteristic of the secular consciousness. To the "devotional" (mystic) schools of yoga, this "unification," obviously, merely precedes true union, the union of the human soul with God.

What is characteristic of yoga is not only its *practical* side but also its *initiatory* structure. One cannot learn yoga alone; one requires the guidance of a *guru* ("teacher"). The yogi begins by renouncing the secular world (family and society) and, guided by his *guru*, he devotes himself to stepping successively beyond all the behavior and values peculiar to the human condition. He endeavors to "die to this life," and it is here that one can best see the initiatory structure of yoga. We are present at a *death* followed by a *rebirth* into another way of being: the way that is represented by deliverance, by access to a way of being that is not profane and that is difficult to describe, which the Indian schools designate under such different names as *moksha, nirvana, asamskrta,* and others.

PATANJALI'S YOGA SUTRAS

Of all the meanings that the word *yoga* possesses in Indian literature, the most exact is the one that deals with yoga "philosophy" (*yoga darsana*) as it is expounded especially in Patanjali's treatise, *Yoga Sutras,* as well as in his commentaries. A *darsana,* obviously, is not a system of philosophy in the Western sense (*darsana* means view, vision, understanding, point of view, doctrine, etc.); it comes from the root *drs* meaning "to see," that is, to contemplate, to understand, etc. But it is nonetheless a system of coherent affirmations coextensive with human experience which it attempts to interpret as a whole, and its aim is "to deliver man from ignorance." In the words of Dr. J. Filliozat:

Strictly *darsana* means *view,* although it is generally translated as *system.* Both versions are justified. *Darsanas* are indeed *views* on the various matters in the domain of philosophy. They are also systems insofar as they constitute coordinated groupings of ideas. Then too they are schools, for most often those who follow them hand down the traditional teaching successively from master to disciple. Above all, the authors who adhere to them seldom compose original works: They annotate the texts accepted as fundamental, or the commentaries on those texts [*L'Inde classique,* II, Paris, 1953, p. 1].

Yoga is one of the six *darsanas,* one of the six Indian orthodox "systems of philosophy" (in this context *orthodox* means tolerated by Brahmanism, in contrast to such heretical systems as, for example, Buddhism or Jainism). And this "classical" yoga, as it was formulated by Patanjali and interpreted by his com-

अथातो योगानुशासनम् ॥ १ ॥

Aph. 1.—Now, then, the exposition of Concentration [is to be made].

a. The expression ' Now, then,' intimates [that] a [distinct]
topic [here commences]; and it serves as a benediction* [—the
particle *atha* being regarded as an auspicious one].

b. The word *yoga*, from the root *yuj* ' to keep the mind fixed
in abstract meditation,' means such a restraining of the exercise
of the mind, or Concentration.†

c. An ' exposition' is that whereby something is expounded, or
declared, through its characteristic marks, its nature, &c. An
' exposition *of the yoga*,'—[such is the meaning of the compound
word] *yogánuśásana*. This [—viz. the expounding of the nature,
&c., of Concentration—] is to be understood to be the topic even
to the end of this Institute‡ [of PATANJALI's].

d. But what *is* Concentration *(yoga)* ? To this he replies :§—

ध्यात्मेवेत्यादिश्रुतिषु मुमुच्चूणां योगविधिरनुष्ठेयत्वेन च्ञेय
तयावगम्यते ऽतो योगविधिमुपदिदिच्चुर्भगवान् पतञ्जलिश्च
व्यावधानाय तच्छास्त्रारमां प्रतिजानीते ॥

* अथशब्दोऽधिकारद्योतको मङ्गलार्थश्च ॥

† युक्तियोगस्समाधानं । युज समाधौ ॥

‡ अनुशिष्यते व्याख्यायते लच्चण्स्वरूपादिभियेन तदनुशा
सनं । योगस्यानुशासनं योगानुशासनम् ।   तदाशास्त्रपरिस
माप्तेरधिकृतं बोद्व्यम् ॥

§ को योग इत्यत आह ॥

mentators, is also the best known in the West. It is appropriate
therefore to begin our discussion with a review of the theories
and practices of yoga as they were formulated by Patanjali in
his *Yoga Sutras*.

The *Yoga Sutras* consist of four chapters or books (*pada*):
the first contains fifty-one aphorisms (sutras) and is the "chapter on yogic escstasy" (*samadhipada*); the second, containing
fifty-five aphorisms, is called *sadhanapada* ("chapter on realization"); the third, which has fifty-five *sutras*, deals with the
"marvelous powers" (*vibhuti*). The fourth and final chapter,
the *kaivalyapada* (*kaivalya*, "isolation") has only thirty-four
sutras and probably represents a later addition. "What could
confirm this hypothesis is the special aspect presented by this
final chapter, which is shorter than the others by almost half
and which goes back to matters already dealt with in the second
chapter or raises others that would have been more appropriate
in one or another of the first three chapters" (Filliozat, *op. cit.*,
II, p. 46).

As for the author of the *Yoga Sutras*, nothing is known of
him. It is not known even whether he lived in the second or the
third century before Christ or even in the fifth century after
Christ. Some Indian commentators, including King Bhoja
(eleventh century), have identified Patanjali, the author of the
Yoga Sutras, with Patanjali the grammarian, who lived in the
first or second century before Christ. The latter was the author
of a "Great Commentary" (*Mahabhashya*) on the famous
grammatical treatise of Panini. The identification of the two
Patanjalis has been accepted by Liebich, Garbe, and S. N.
Dasgupta and challenged by Woods, H. Jacobi, and A. B.
Keith. These last two scholars have found traces of anti-
Buddhist polemic in the sixth chapter of the *Yoga Sutras*, as a
consequence of which it would hardly be possible to date
Patanjali earlier than the fifth century. But Jvala Prasad has
shown that sutra iv, 16—in which one could find an allusion
to the Buddhism of the Yogacaras—is not part of the text of
Patanjali. This sutra merely repeats a line in the commentary of

Patanjali's *Yoga Sutras*: bilingual Sanskrit-English edition, Allahabad, 1852

Vyasa (seventh century), in which he disputes with the Vijnanavadins. Besides, King Bhoja had already observed that this
sutra was an interpolation by Vyasa, and therefore he did not
comment on it. Furthermore, Jvala Prasad and Dasgupta point
out that, even if the authors discussed in this sutra are the
Vijnanavadins, we have no reason to believe that it refers to
authors as late as Vasubandhu or Asanga. The text could equally
well be related to a more ancient idealist school such as those
found in the first Upanishads.

Regardless where the truth may actually lie, these controversies over the age of the *Yoga Sutras* are of rather minor
importance, for the techniques of asceticism and meditation
elaborated by Patanjali are certainly of great antiquity; they
are not his discoveries or those of his time; they had been put to
the test many centuries before him. The Indian authors, besides,
seldom propose individual systems; in the great majority of
cases they are satisfied to present the traditional doctrines in the
language of their own periods. This can be verified in even more
typical fashion in the case of Patanjali, whose sole aim was to
compile a practical handbook of very ancient techniques. Nor is
it impossible that the original text of the *Yoga Sutras* may have
been revised by many hands in order to adapt it to new "philosophical situations."

As was the case with the other *darsanas*, the basic treatise
was meditated and commented on by many authors. The earliest
work known to us is the *Yogabhashya* of Vyasa (sixth and
seventh centuries). This commentary was annotated in its turn
by Vacaspati Misra about A.D. 850 in his *Tattvavaisaradi*. These
two texts are ranked among the most important contributions
to an understanding of the *Yoga Sutras*. King Bhoja (early
eleventh century) was the author of the commentary entitled
Rajamartanda, which is very useful for its insights into certain
yogic practices. "It was perhaps through this commentary, which
was then quite new, that Al-Buruni was initiated into Patanjali's
Yoga, on which, moreover, he wrote a book in Arabic"
(Filliozat, *op. cit.*). Finally Vijnanabhikshu (sixteenth century)

wrote a commentary on Vyasa's *Yogabhashya* in his treatise, *Yogavarttika,* which is remarkable from every point of view. (More editions and translations of yogic texts are listed in the bibliography, p. 205.)

SAMKHYA AND YOGA

Patanjali himself acknowledged (Y.S., I, i) that in sum he was merely publishing and correcting the doctrinal and technical traditions of yoga. The closed circles of the Indian ascetics and mystics, in fact, knew the yogic practices long before Patanjali's

Kapila, regarded by Isvara Krishna as the founder of the Samkhya system (eighth-century sculpture at Anuradhapura, Ceylon)

time. Of the technical prescriptions preserved by tradition Patanjali retained those that had been adequately verified by age-old practice. Patanjali's personal contribution with respect to the theoretical framework and the metaphysical foundation that he gave to these practices was minimal. He merely repeated, in its broad outlines, the Samkhya philosophy, which he coordinated with a rather superficial theism. Yoga and Samkhya philosophical systems resembled each other so closely that most of the statements of either were equally valid for the other. The basic differences between them were few:

1. Whereas Samkhya was atheistic, yoga was theistic, since it postulated the existence of a supreme God (Isvara).

2. While according to Samkhya the only route to salvation is that of metaphysical knowledge, yoga granted considerable importance to the techniques of meditation.

In sum, what can properly be called Patanjali's work was directed principally to the coordination of the philosophical material—borrowed from Samkhya—with the technical prescriptions for concentration, meditation, and ecstasy. Thanks to Patanjali, yoga was advanced from a "mystic" tradition to the level of a "system of philosophy."

Indian tradition regards Samkhya as the most ancient *darsana*. The meaning of the name seems to have been "discrimination," since the chief purpose of this philosophy was to dissociate the spirit (*purusha*) from matter (*prakrti*). The most ancient treatise is the *Samkhya Karika* of Isvara Krishna; its date has not yet been definitively established but in no event can it be later than the fifth century after Christ. Among the commentaries on the *Samkhya Karika* the most valuable is *Samkhya-tatva-kaumudi*, by Vacaspati Misra (sixteenth century). Another important commentary is *Samkhya-pravacana-Sutra* (probably fourteenth century) with the commentaries of Aniruddha (fifteenth century) and Vijnanabhikshu (sixteenth century).

Certainly the importance of the chronology of the Samkhya texts must not be exaggerated. In general, any Indian philosophical treatise contains conceptions anterior to the date of its composition, and often very ancient ones. If one encounters a new interpretation in a philosophical text, that does not mean that it had not been envisaged earlier. Too much importance has been given to the allusions and the controversies that it may be possible to unearth in these philosophical texts. The objects of these references may well have been much older views than those to which they are apparently addressed. Although it is occasionally possible to fix the date at which a given manuscript was written, it is much more difficult to establish a chronology for the philosophical ideas themselves. Exactly like yoga, Samkhya too has a prehistory. Very probably the origin of the system ought to be sought in the analysis of the constituent elements of human experience with a view to distinguishing between those that leave man when he dies and those that are "immortal" in the sense that they accompany the soul in its destiny beyond the grave. Such an analysis was already to be found in the Satapatha Brahmana (X, 1, 3, 4), which divided the human being into three "immortal" parts and three mortal parts. In other words, the "origins" of Samkhya are linked to a problem of a mystic nature: *What survives of man after death? What constitutes the veritable Self, the immortal element in the human being?*

"CREATIVE NOT-KNOWING"

In Samkhya and yoga the world is *real* (not *illusory*, as it is for example in the Vedanta). Nevertheless, although the world *exists* and *endures*, it owes this to the "ignorance" of the spirit: The innumerable forms of the cosmos, as well as their methods of manifestation and development, exist only to the degree to which the spirit, the Self (*purusha*), is ignorant of itself and, by reason of this ignorance of a metaphysical nature, suffers and is subjugated. At the exact instant when the last Self shall have found its freedom, the whole of creation will be reabsorbed into the primordial substance.

It is in this fundamental affirmation (more or less explicitly stated), according to which the cosmos exists and endures through man's not-knowing, that the motivation can be found for the depreciation of life and the cosmos; a depreciation that none of the great constructions of post-Vedic Indian thought has attempted to conceal. Beginning at the time of the Upanishads, India has rejected the world *as it is* and devaluated life as it reveals itself to the eyes of the wise: ephemeral, anguished, illusory. Such a conception leads neither to nihilism nor to pessimism. One rejects *this* world and depreciates *this* life because one knows that there exists *something else,* beyond growth, beyond temporality, beyond suffering. In religious terms it might almost be said that India rejects the cosmos and *profane* life because she thirsts for a *sacred* world and way of life.

The Indian texts reiterate, to the point of satiation, this thesis according to which the cause of the soul's "enslavement" and, consequently, the source of sufferings without end, lie in *man's solidarity with the cosmos,* in his active or passive, direct or indirect participation in Nature. Translation: solidarity with a world *that has lost its sanctity,* participation in a *profane* Nature. *Neti! Neti!* the wise man of the Upanishads cries: "No! No! You are not *this,* and no more are you *that!*" In other words: you are not part of the degraded cosmos *as you see it now,* you are not necessarily drawn into *this Creation* (*srshti*); *necessarily* means in terms of the inherent law of your being. For *being* can never maintain any relation with *nonbeing.* Now Nature has no true ontological reality; it is in effect a universal process of becoming. Every cosmic form, however complex and majestic it may be, in the end disintegrates; the universe itself is periodically reabsorbed by "great dissolutions" (*mahapralaya*) into the primordial matrix (*prakrti*). Now whatever becomes, is transformed, dies, and disappears is not part of the sphere of being. Let us translate once again: Therefore it is not *sacred.* If solidarity with the cosmos is the result of a progressive desanctification of human existence

and is therefore a plunge into ignorance and sorrow, the road to freedom necessarily leads to a *desolidarization* with the cosmos and profane life. (In certain forms of Tantrist Yoga this divorce is followed by a desperate attempt to *resanctify* existence.)

And yet the cosmos and life have an ambivalent function. On the one hand, they thrust man into suffering and, through karma, incorporate him into the infinite cycle of transmigrations; on the other hand, they help him indirectly to seek and find the "salvation" of his soul, autonomy, absolute freedom (*moksha, mukti*). The more man suffers, in fact—that is, the more he is bound with the cosmos—the more he is filled with the thirst for salvation. Thus—and thanks to the suffering that their evolution indefatigably aliments—cosmic forms and illusions enlist in the service of man, whose supreme purpose is emancipation, salvation. "From Brahma to a blade of grass, the Creation [*srshti*] is for the soul's benefit, until one attains to the supreme knowledge" (S.S., III, 47). The supreme knowledge means emancipation not only from ignorance but also and even first of all from anguish, from suffering.

UNIVERSAL SUFFERING

"All is suffering for the wise man," Patanjali wrote (*Y.S.*, II, 15). But Patanjali was neither the first nor the last to take cognizance of universal suffering. Long before, Buddha had proclaimed: "All is anguish, all is ephemeral." This is a leitmotiv of all Indian post-Upanishad speculation. The redemptive techniques, as well as the metaphysical doctrines, found their basic origin in this univeral suffering; for they are of value only in the measure to which they deliver man from "suffering." Human experience, whatever its character, engenders suffering. "The body is pain because it is the seat of pain; the senses, objects, perceptions are suffering, because they lead to suffering; even pleasure is suffering because it is followed by suffering" (Aniruddha, commenting on S.S., II, 1). And Isvara Krishna,

the author of the most ancient Samkhya treatise, asserts that
at the foundation of this philosophy there is man's desire to
escape the torture of the three anguishes: heavenly suffering
(provoked by the gods), earthly suffering (caused by Nature),
and inner or organic suffering (S.K., I).

And yet this universal suffering does not lead to a "pessimist
philosophy." No Indian philosophy and no Indian gnosis found-
ers in despair. The revelation of "suffering" as the law of
existence can be regarded, on the contrary, as the *conditio
sine qua non* of liberation; this universal suffering, then, has
an intrinsic positive, stimulating value. Unceasingly it reminds
the sage and the ascetic that they have only one means of attaining to freedom and beatitude: withdrawal from the world,
detachment from wealth and ambition, radical self-isolation.
Moreover, it is not man alone who suffers; suffering is a cosmic
necessity, an ontological modality to which every "form" that
manifests itself as such is dedicated. Whether one be a god
or a minuscule insect, the mere fact of existing in time, of
having a term, implies suffering. In contrast to the gods and
other living beings, man has the possibility of effectively rising
above his condition and thus abolishing suffering. The certainty
of the existence of a means of putting an end to suffering—a
certainty common to all Indian philosophies and mysticisms—
cannot lead to "despair" or to "pessimism." Suffering, it is
true, is universal; but, if one knows how to comport oneself
in order to be free of it, it is not final. In fact, although the
human condition is in pledge to suffering for eternity—in so
far as this is determined, like every condition, by karma—
every individual who shares this condition may rise beyond it,
since everyone can nullify the forces of karma that govern it.
(Let us recall the meanings of the word karma: work; action;
destiny—the ineluctable consequence of acts performed in an
earlier existence—product, effect, etc.)

To "liberate oneself" from suffering is the goal of all the
philosophies and mysticisms of India. Whether this deliverance
is gained directly through "knowledge," as the Vedanta and

Universal suffering

Indifference to property and ambition

Samkhya, for example, teach, or through the use of techniques, as the majority of the Buddhist schools, like yoga, believes, the fact remains that no learning has value if its object is not the "salvation" of man. "Beyond that nothing is worth knowing," the Svetasvatara Upanishad says (I, 12). And Bhoja, discussing a passage in the *Yoga Sutras* (IV, 22), declared that knowledge whose object was not deliverance was barren of all worth. Vacaspati Misra began his commentary on Isvara Krishna's treatise thus:

In this world the hearer listens only to the speaker who deals with facts the knowledge of which is necessary and desired. No one pays attention to those who expound doctrines that no one wants, as is the case with madmen or with ordinary men who are good at their practical affairs but ignorant of the sciences and the arts [*Tattva-Kaumudi*, published by G. Jha, Bombay, 1896, p. 1].

The same author, in his commentary on the Vedantasutra-bhashya, specifies what knowledge is needed: "No lucid person wishes to know what is naked of all certainty or what is of no usefulness . . . or of no importance" (*Bhamati*, published by Jivananda-vidyasagara Bhattacharyya, Calcutta, pp. 1–2).

THE REDEMPTIVE FUNCTION OF KNOWLEDGE

Metaphysical knowledge has always had a soteriological purpose in India. Therefore only metaphysical knowledge (*vidya, jnana, prajna*) is appreciated and sought after—that is, knowledge of the ultimate realities; for it alone procures deliverance. It is indeed through "knowledge" that, freeing himself from the illusions of the world of phenomena, man "awakens." *Through knowledge* means through the practice of withdrawal, the effect of which will be to enable man to find his own center, to make him coincide with his "real spirit" (*purusha, atman*). Knowledge is thus transformed into meditation and metaphysics becomes soteriology.

The practice of retreat (second-century sculpture)

The considerable importance given to "knowledge" by all Indian metaphysicians, including that technique of asceticism and method of meditation known as yoga, is easily understood if one takes into account the causes of human suffering. The misery of human life is due not to divine punishment or to original sin but to *ignorance*. Not simply ignorance in general, but only ignorance of the true nature of the *spirit*, the ignorance that makes us confuse the spirit with psychomental experience, that causes us to attribute "qualities" and characteristics to that eternal, autonomous principle that is the spirit; in short, ignorance of a metaphysical kind. It was therefore natural that it should be a metaphysical knowledge that would extirpate that ignorance. This knowledge of a metaphysical kind leads the disciple to the threshold of illumination—that is, to his true "Self." And it is this knowledge of oneself—not in the secular sense but in the ascetic and spiritual meaning of the phrase— that is the goal sought by a large proportion of Indian specula-

tion even though each form taken by that speculation points
to a different road by which it is to be achieved.

For Samkhya and yoga the problem is precise. Since the
origin of suffering is the "ignorance" of the spirit—that is, the
fact that the "spirit" is confused with psychomental states—
release can be obtained only by eliminating this confusion. The
differences that separate Samkhya from yoga on this point are
minor. Only the methods are really different: Samkhya seeks
to obtain deliverance through *gnosis* alone, whereas for yoga
asceticism and a *meditative technique* are indispensable. In both
darsanas, human suffering has its origin in an illusion; man
believes, in effect, that his psychomental life—the activity of
his senses, emotions, thoughts and desires—is identical with
the spirit, the Self. Thus he confuses two wholly autonomous
and opposing realities, between which there is no real connection but only illusory relations, for psychomental experience
does not belong to the spirit: It belongs to Nature (*prakrti*).
States of consciousness are the refined products of the same
substance that is at the basis of the physical world and the
world of life. Between psychic states and inanimate objects or
living beings the only differences are those of degree. But, between psychic states and the spirit, there is a difference of an
ontological character: They belong to two distinct modes of
being. "Deliverance" appears when this truth has been grasped
and when the spirit regains its original freedom.

Thus, according to Samkhya, he who seeks to win emancipation should begin by thoroughly learning the essence and the
forms of Nature (*prakrti*) and the laws that govern its evolution. Yoga, on the other hand, also accepts this analysis of substance but it attributes value only to the practice of contemplation, which alone has the capacity to reveal experimentally the
autonomy of the spirit's omnipotence. Hence it is appropriate,
before taking up the methods and techniques of yoga, to see
how the Samkhya *darsana* conceives of substance and spirit, as
well as the cause of their false solidarity; to see in short exactly
what constitutes the gnostic path called for by this "philosophy."

It is also necessary to determine to what extent the doctrines of Samkhya and yoga coincide and to distinguish, in the theoretical statements of the latter *darsana*, those that derive from "mystic" experiences that are lacking to Samkhya.

THE "SELF"

The spirit (the "soul")—as a transcendent, autonomous principle—is accepted by all the Indian philosophies except Buddhism and materialism. But the roads are very varied by which the different *darsanas* attempt to prove its existence and explain its essence. To the Nyaya school the soul-spirit is an entity without characteristics, absolute, unconscious. The Vedanta, on the other hand, defines the *atman* as being *saccidananda* (*sat*, "being"; *cit*, "consciousness"; *ananda*, "blessedness") and regards the spirit as a unique, universal, eternal reality dramatically enmeshed in the temporal illusion of the Creation (*maya*). Samkhya and yoga deny the spirit (*purusha*) any attribute and any relation; all that can be said on the subject of the spirit, according to both *darsanas*, is that it *is* and that it *knows* (here, of course, we are dealing with that metaphysical knowledge that results from the contemplation of its own way of being).

Quite like the *atman* of the Upanishads, the *purusha* is inexpressible. Its "attributes" are negative. "The spirit is what sees [*sakshin*, witness], it is isolated [*kaivalyam*], indifferent, a mere inactive spectator," Isvara Krishna wrote (S.K., 19); and Gaudapada insisted in his commentary on the eternal passivity of the *purusha*. Autonomy and impassibility are traditional epithets for the spirit. Since it is irreducible and devoid of qualities, the *purusha* has no "intelligence" (S.S., I, 146), for it is without desires. Desires are not eternal and hence they are not part of the spirit. The spirit is eternally free (S.S., I, 162), for "states of consciousness" and the flux of the psychomental life are foreign to it. If nevertheless the *purusha* appears to us to be an "agent" (*kartr*), that is the result as much of human illusion as of that proximity *sui generis* that is called

yogyata and that designates a kind of preestablished harmony between those two essentially distinct realities, the Self (*purusha*) and the intelligence (*buddhi*), since, as we shall see presently, the latter is merely a "more refined product" of primordial substance.

Patanjali takes the same position. In the *Yoga Sutras*, II, 5, he points out that ignorance consists in regarding what is ephemeral, impure, painful, and non-spirit as being eternal, pure blessedness and spirit. Vyasa (*Y.S.* II, 18) specifies once again that perception, memory, reason, etc., are in fact part of the intelligence (*buddhi*) and that it is solely as the result of an illusion that these mental faculties are ascribed to the *purusha*.

Now this conception of the *purusha* incites difficulties from the outset. If indeed the spirit is eternally pure, impassible, autonomous, and irreducible, how can it consent to allow itself to be accompanied by psychomental experience? And how is such a relation possible? We shall derive more profit from an examination of the solution to this problem proposed by Samkhya and yoga when we understand better the relations that can exist between the Self and Nature. At that time we shall see that the work of both *darsanas* bears chiefly on the problem of the true nature of this strange "relation" that links the *purusha* to *prakrti*. But neither the *origin* nor the *cause* of this paradoxical situation has been the subject of any formal discussion between Samkhya and yoga. Why indeed has the Self consented to let itself be drawn into a strange orbit, particularly that of Life, and thus to engender man as such, concrete, historic man committed to every drama, at grips with every anguish? When and on what occasion did this tragedy of man's existence begin if it is true that the ontological modality of the spirit is, as we have already seen, exactly the opposite of the human condition, since the Self is eternal, free, and passive?

The *cause* and the *origin* of this association of spirit and experience are two aspects of a problem that Samkhya and yoga view as insoluble because it exceeds the present capacity of

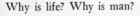

Why is life? Why is man?

human understanding. In fact man knows and understands through the medium of what Samkhya and yoga call the "intellect" (*buddhi*). But this "intellect" is itself only a product—extremely refined, it is true—of primordial substance (*prakti*). Since it is a product of Nature, a "phenomenon," the *buddhi* can have relations of knowledge only with other phenomena (which, like itself, are members of the infinite series of the creations of primordial substance); in no event would it be able to know the Self, for it would be incapable of maintaining relations of any kind with a transcendental reality. Only some instrument of knowledge other than the *buddhi*, in no way implying the material, would be able to succeed in understanding the cause as well as the origin of this paradoxical association of Self and Life (that is, "matter"). Now such knowledge is impossible to the present human condition. It is "revealed" only to him who has gone beyond the human condition: The "intellect" has no part in this revelation, which is, rather, knowledge of oneself, of the Self itself.

Samkhya knows that the cause of "servitude"—in other words the human condition, suffering—is metaphysical ignorance, which, by reason of the law of karma, is transmitted from one existence to another; but the historical moment at which this ignorance made its appearance cannot be established, just as it is impossible to settle the date of the Creation. The connection between Self and Life, as well as the "servitude" that follows from it (for the Self), has no history; both are beyond time, they are eternal. To try to find solutions to these problems is not only a futile effort but infantile. These problems have been badly stated, and, according to an old Brahman custom invoked by Buddha himself on a number of occasions, the reply to a badly stated problem is silence. The only certainty possible on this subject is that man has been in this condition since the most remote eras and that the goal of knowledge is not the vain investigation of the First Cause and the historic origins of this condition but deliverance.

SUBSTANCE AND STRUCTURES

Patanjali refers in passing to *prakrti* (*Y.S.*, 2, 3) and its modalities, the *gunas* (*Y.S.*, I, 16; II, 15, 19; IV, 13, 34, 32), but solely in order to state precisely their relations with psychomental life and with the techniques of deliverance. He assumes the reader's knowledge of the analysis of substance arduously carried through by the Samkhya authors.

Prakrti is as real and as eternal as the *purusha,* but, in contrast to the spirit, it is dynamic and creative. Although it is completely homogeneous and inert, this primordial substance might be said to possess three "ways of being," which enable it to manifest itself in three different fashions and which are called *gunas:* the first is *sattva,* the modality of luminosity and intelligence; the second is *rajas,* the modality of motor energy and mental activity; and the third is *tamas,* the modality of static inertia and psychic obscurity. Nevertheless these *gunas* cannot be regarded as being different from *prakrti,* because they are never manifested individually; in every physical, biological, or psychomental phenomenon all three are present at once, although in unequal proportions. (It is precisely this inequality that makes possible the appearance of a "phenomenon," whatever its nature; otherwise the equilibrium and the primordial homogeneity as a result of which the *gunas* were in perfect balance would persist eternally.) It is apparent that the *gunas* have a dual nature: on the one hand, objective, since they constitute the phenomena of the external world; on the other hand, subjective, because they support, nourish, and condition psychomental life. (That is why *tamas* ought to be translated both as "principle of the inertia of matter," the objective sense, and "obscurity of consciousness, obstacle created by the passions," the psychophysiological sense.)

As soon as it emerges from its original state of perfect equilibrium (*alinga, avyakta*) and assumes characteristics conditioned by its "teleological instinct" (to which we shall return), *prakrti* appears in the form of a mass of energy called *mahat* ("the great"). Carried along by the pressure of evolution (*parinama*, "development," progress), *prakrti* proceeds from the state of *mahat* to that of *ahamkara*, which means an apperceptive unitary mass still devoid of "personal" experience but endowed with the obscure consciousness of being an ego (whence the term *ahamkara*, since *aham* means "ego"). Starting with this apperceptive mass, the process of "evolution" bifurcates in two opposing directions, of which one leads to the world of objective phenomena and the other to that of subjective phenomena (perceivable and psychomental).

Ahamkara has the faculty of qualitative transformation in accordance with that one of the three *gunas* that is predominant. When it is *sattva* (the modality of luminosity, purity, and understanding) that dominates within *ahamkara*, it is the five cognitive senses (*jnanendriya*) and "the inner sense" (*manas*) that emerge; this inner sense serves as a connection between perceptive and biomotor activity; the basis and the recipient of all impressions, it coordinates the biological and psychological activities, especially that of the subconscious. When, on the other hand, the equilibrium is dominated by *rajas* (motor energy, which makes possible every physical or cognitive experience), it is the five conative senses (*karmendriya*) that emerge. Finally, when it is *tamas* (the inertia of matter, the obscurity of consciousness, the barrier of the passions) that dominates, it is the five "rarefied" (potential) elements, *tanmatra*, the genetic nuclei of the physical world, that appear. From these *tanmatra*, through a process of condensation that tends to produce increasingly coarser structures, are derived the atoms (*paramanu*) and the molecules (*sthutabhutani*, literally "dense material particle"), which in turn give birth to the vegetable and animal organisms. Thus man's body, as well as his "states of consciousness" and even his "intelligence," is the creation of the same single substance.

It will be observed that, according to Samkhya and yoga, the universe—objective or subjective—is merely the development of an initial stage of Nature, *ahamkara*, in which for the first time the consciousness of individuality, of apperception illuminated by the ego, surges up out of the homogeneous mass of energy. By means of a dual process of development and creation, *ahamkara* has created a double universe: inner and outer, these two "worlds" having optional connections with each other. Each sense corresponds to a specific atom, just as each atom corresponds to a *tanmatra*. But each of these products contains the three *gunas*, though in unequal ratio; each product is characterized by the supremacy of one *guna* or, in the final stages of creation, by the predominance of one *tanmatra*.

It is important to understand the idea of "evolution" in Samkhya. *Parinama* means the development of what potentially exists in the *mahat*. This is not a creation, an excess, or the realization of new species of existence, but simply the actualization of the potentialities existing in *prakrti* (in its living aspect, *mahat*). To compare "evolution" in the Indian sense with Western evolution would be to create immeasurable confusion. No new form, Samkhya declares, exceeds the possibilities of existence that were already in being in the universe. In Samkhya, in fact, nothing is created in the Western sense of the word. Creation has existed since all eternity and can never be destroyed, but it will revert to its original quality of absolute equilibrium (in the great ultimate reabsorption, *mahapralaya*).

Isvara Krishna defined *ahamkara* as "the knowledge of self" (*S.K.*, 24). This entity, although "material," does not manifest itself in sensory, physical forms; it is homogeneous, a pure mass of energy without any structure. According to Samkhya, *ahamkara* becomes conscious of itself and, by this process, it is reflected through the range of the eleven psychic principles (*manas*, or the inner sense that coordinates the faculties of the soul, the five cognitive senses, and the five conative senses) and the range of the physical powers (*tanmatra*).

There is good reason to note the prime importance that Samkhya, like almost all the Indian systems, ascribes to the *principle of individuation through "consciousness of self."* It

will be observed that the genesis of the world is a psychic act
and that the evolution of the physical world is derived from this
"consciousness of self" (which, of course, is absolutely different
from the "awakening" of the *purusha*). Objective and psychophysiological phenomena have a common matrix, the only difference that separates them being the *formula* of the *gunas:*
sattva dominating in psychic phenomena, *rajas* in psychophysiological phenomena (passion, sensory activity, etc.), while
the phenomena of "matter" are composed of the increasingly
inert and dense products of *tamas* (*tanmatra, anu, bhutani*).

Samkhya and yoga also offer a subjective interpretation of
the three *gunas* when their psychic "aspects" are considered. To
Patanjali, when it is *sattva* that is predominant, consciousness
is calm, clear, comprehensible, and virtuous; dominated by *rajas*,
it is agitated, unsure, unstable; overwhelmed by *tamas*, it is
obscure, confused, excited, and bestial (see Y.S., II, 15, 19,
with commentaries). But naturally this subjective, human
evaluation of the three cosmic modalities does not contradict
their objective character, inasmuch as "outer" and "inner" are
mere words.

With this physiological foundation it is understandable why
Samkhya and yoga regard every psychic experience as a mere
"material" process. This is reflected in their morality: Purity,
goodness are not qualities of the spirit but a "purification" of
the "subtle matter" represented by consciousness. The *gunas*
impregnate the whole universe and establish an organic sympathy between man and the cosmos, both these entities being
penetrated by the same anguish of existence and both serving
the same absolute Self, alien to the world and impelled by an
unguessable destiny. In fact the difference between cosmos and
man is a difference only of degree, not of essence.

THE TELEOLOGICAL NATURE OF THE CREATION

Thanks to *parinama*, matter has produced infinite forms
increasingly combined, increasingly varied. Samkhya believes

The yogi between *purusha* (symbolized by the sacred syllable OM) and *prakrti* (reflected by the five senses). A modern popular drawing

that so vast a creation, so complicated a construction of forms
and organisms, requires a justification and a significance beyond
itself. A primordial *prakrti*, formless and eternal, can mean
something. But the world as we see it is not a homogeneous substance; on the contrary, it offers a great number of distinct
structures and forms. The complexity of the cosmos, the in-
finiteness of its "forms" are raised by Samkhya to the rank of
metaphysical arguments. The "Creation" is beyond question
the product of our metaphysical ignorance; the existence of the
universe and the polymorphism of life are the result of man's
false opinion of himself of the fact that he confuses the real
Self with psychomental states. But, as we remarked earlier, it
is impossible to know what are the origin and the cause of this
false opinion. What is known, what is seen, is that *prakrti* has
a most complicated evolution and that it is not simple but
"compounded."

Now common sense tells us that every compound exists by
reason of another. So, for instance, a bed is a whole composed
of several parts, but this temporary collaboration among the
parts does not have an order of its own, it is imposed by man
(*S.K.*, 17, with commentaries, Vacaspati Misra, 120; *S.S.*, I,
140–144, with commentaries by Aniruddha and by Vijnana
Bhikshu). Thus Samkhya brings out the *teleological character
of the Creation*; if indeed it were not the mission of the Creation to serve the spirit, it would be absurd, barren of meaning.
Everything in Nature is compounded; everything then should
have a "superviser" (*adhyakshah*), someone who can make
use of these components. It would be impossible for this "superviser" to be mental activity or states of consciousness (themselves the extremely complex products of *prakrti*). Therefore
there ought to be an entity that goes beyond the categories of
substance (*guna*) and that is imposed by itself (Vacaspati
Misra, 122, on *S.K.*, 17). Better still, there ought to exist someone to whom mental activity is subordinated, toward whom
"pleasure and pain" are oriented. For, Misra adds (123), it
would be impossible for pleasure to be felt and distinguished

What happens to us is not part of us

through pleasure; and, if it were felt through pain, it would be no longer a pleasurable but a painful experience. Thus the two qualities (pain and pleasure) can exist and can be distinguished only as they are directed toward a single subject beyond experience.

This is the first proof of the existence of the spirit that Samkhya discovered: "The knowledge of the existence of the spirit through combination for the profit of others," an axiom abundantly reiterated in Indian literature (S.S., I, 66; Vacaspati Misra on S.K., 17; Brhadaranyaka Up., II, 4, 5) and appropriated by yoga (cf. Y.S., IV, 24). Misra adds that, if it should be objected that the purpose of the evolution and the heterogeneity of substance is to serve other "compounds" (as is the case, for example, of the bed, since this "compound" is created with a view to that other "compound," the human body), it can be

argued in reply that these compounds too must exist in their
turn in order that other compounds make use of them. The
series of interdependences would inevitably lead us to a *regressus
ad infinitum*. "And," Vacaspati Misra continues, "since we can
avoid this *regressus* by postulating the existence of a rational
Principle, it obviously makes no sense uselessly to multiply the
series of relationships among compounds" (*Tattva-Kaumudi*,
121). In conformity with this postulate, the spirit, the Self, is
a simple, irreducible principle, autonomous, static, unproduc-
tive, unimplicated in mental or sensory activity, etc.

Although the Self (*purusha*) is veiled by the illusions and
confusions of the cosmic Creation, *prakrti* is galvanized by that
"teleological instinct" wholly directed to the "deliverance" of
the *purusha*. Let us remember that "from Brahma to the lowest
blade of grass the Creation is for the benefit of the spirit until
it has attained to supreme knowledge" (*S.S.*, III, 47).

THE SPIRIT-NATURE RELATION

Although the philosophies of Samkhya and yoga do not explain the reason or the origin of the strange association that has
been established between the spirit and experience, they do
endeavor nevertheless to explain the nature of their association
and to define the character of their mutual relations. It is not a
matter of *real* relations in the strict sense of the word, such as
the relations that exist, for example, between external objects
and perceptions. Real relations in fact imply change and plurality; but here we have modalities basically opposed to the nature
of the spirit.

"States of consciousness" are only products of *prakrti*, and
they cannot maintain any kind of relations with the spirit,
which, by reason of its very essence, is above all experience. But
—and, for Samkhya and yoga, this is the key to this paradoxical
situation—the most subtle, the most transparent part of mental
life (that is, the intelligence, *buddhi*, in its form of pure
"luminosity," *sattva*) has a specific faculty: that of reflecting

the spirit. Comprehension of the external world is possible only by reason of this reflection of the *purusha* in the intelligence. But the Self is not altered by this reflection and it does not lose its ontological modalities (impassibility, eternity, etc.).

The *Yoga Sutras* (II, 20) say in substance that the seer (*drashtr*, in other words the *purusha*) is absolute consciousness ("vision at its highest") and, even while he preserves his purity, he knows all knowledges (he "considers the ideas that are offered to him"). Vyasa interprets this: The spirit is reflected in the intelligence (*buddhi*), but it is neither like nor unlike the intelligence. It is not like the intelligence because the intelligence is changed by knowledge of objects, which itself is constantly changing, whereas the *purusha* possesses unbroken knowledge and in some way it *is* knowledge. On the other hand, the *purusha* is not wholly unlike the *buddhi* because, although it is pure, it knows knowledge. Patanjali employs another image to make explicit the relations between the spirit and the intelligence: Just as a flower is reflected in a glass, the intelligence reflects the *purusha* (cf. Y.S., I, 41). But only the ignorant could attribute the qualities of the flower (form, size, colors) to the glass. When the object (the flower) dies, its reflection in the glass dies even though the glass remains unaltered. It is an illusion to think that the spirit is dynamic because mental experience is. In reality this is a question merely of an illusory relation (*upadhi*) resulting from a "sympathetic correspondence" (*yogyata*) between the Self and the intelligence.

Through all eternity the spirit is drawn into this illusory relation with psychomental life (that is, with "matter"). This is the result of ignorance, *avidya* (Y.S., II, 24), and, as long as *avidya* endures, existence is there by reason of karma, and with it there is suffering. Let us stress this point to a degree. Illusion or ignorance consists in the confusion between the unmoving, eternal *purusha* and the flux of psychomental life (S.S., III, 41). To say *I am suffering, I want, I hate, I know,* and to think that this *I* has to do with the spirit is to live in illusion and keep it alive; for all our actions or intentions, by the simple fact that they can be justified by *prakrti*, by "matter," are conditioned and directed by karma. This means that every action that has its origin in illusion (in other words, that is founded on *ignorance*, confusion between spirit and non-spirit) is either the consummation of a potential created by an earlier act or the projection of another power that in turn demands its actualization, its consummation in this existence or in some future existence. When one sets up the equation "I want = the spirit wants," a certain force is thus set loose or else another has been engendered. For the confusion of which this equation is the expression is a "moment" in the eternal circuit of the cosmic energies.

This is the law of existence; it is transsubjective like any law, but its validity and its universality are at the source of the suffering to which life is attached. There is only one sole way of obtaining salvation: to know the spirit sufficiently. Samkhya merely continues the tradition of the Upanishads: "He who knows the *atman* crosses [the ocean of suffering]" (Chandogya Up., VII, i, 3). "Through knowledge, deliverance; through ignorance, enslavement" (*S.S.*, III, 22, 23). And the first stage in the conquest of this "knowledge" consists in this: denying that the spirit has attributes. This comes back to denying suffering insofar as it concerns us, to regarding it as an objective fact, external to the spirit, in other words *stripped of value*, of *meaning* (since all "values" and all "meanings" are created by the intelligence insofar as it reflects the *purusha*). Pain exists only in the degree in which experience is related to the human personality regarded as identical with the *purusha*, with the Self. But, since this relation is illusory, it can easily be abolished. When the *purusha* is known, *values* are nullified; pain then is no longer pain or non-pain, but a mere *fact*; a "fact" that, even while it retains the sensory structure, loses its value, its meaning.

It is most essential to understand this point, which is of prime importance to the doctrines of Samkhya and yoga and on which, in my opinion, there has not been sufficient emphasis. In order to be delivered from pain, Samkhya and yoga *deny*

suffering as such, thus eliminating all relation between suffering
and the Self. As soon as we understand that the Self is free,
eternal, and inactive, everything that happens to us—pain,
emotion, desire, thought, etc.—*is no longer a part of us.* It is all
a complex of cosmic facts conditioned by laws that are assuredly
real but whose reality has nothing in common with our *purusha.*
Pain is a cosmic fact, and man endures this fact or contributes
to its perpetuation solely to the extent to which he allows himself to be lured by an illusion.

Knowledge is a simple "awakening" that unveils the essence
of the Self, of the spirit. Knowledge "produces" nothing—it is
an immediate revelation of reality. This genuine, absolute
knowledge—it should not be confused with intellectual activity,
which is psychological in its nature—is gained not by experience
but by revelation. There is no divine intervention here, for
Samkhya denies the existence of God; yoga accepts God, but
we shall see that Patanjali did not ascribe any great importance
to this. Revelation is founded on the knowledge of ultimate
reality—that is, on that "awakening" in which object is completely identified with subject. (The Self "contemplates" itself;
it does not "think" itself, because thinking is itself an experience and, as such, it is part of *prakrti.*)

HOPE IS THE GREATEST TORTURE

To Samkhya no road other than this exists. Hope indeed pro-
longs and aggravates human misery; only he who has lost all
hope is happy (*S.S.,* IV, ii), "for hope is the greatest torture
that exists and despair is the great happiness" (from the
Mahabharata, quoted in Mahadeva Vedantin's commentary on
S.S., IV, ii). Religious rituals and observances are of no value
(*S.S.,* III, 26), because they are based on desires and cruelties.
Any ritual action, for the very reason that it entails an effort,
engenders a new force of karma (*S.S.,* I, 84–85). Even morality
leads to nothing decisive. Indifference (*vairagya,* meaning
"renunciation"), orthodoxy (*sruti*), and meditation are only

indirect instruments of salvation. The sole perfect, conclusive means, to Samkhya, is metaphysical knowledge (*S.S.*, III, 23).

The cognitive process is of course carried through by the intellect; but this is a highly advanced form of "matter." How then is it possible to achieve deliverance (*mukti*) through the collaboration of *prakrti*? Samkhya's reply is the teleological argument: matter (*prakrti*) acts instinctively toward the end of the liberation of the "spirit" (*purusha*). Intellect (*buddhi*), being the most perfect manifestation of *prakrti*, is able through its dynamic capabilities to facilitate the process of deliverance by serving as an initial steppingstone to revelation. Patanjali took exactly the same position (cf. *Y.S.*, II, 18, etc.): *prakrti* makes experience possible and at the same time pursues the deliverance of the Self. In his commentary on this sutra Vyasa added an important clarification: In fact, he said, enslavement is nothing but the situation of the intelligence (*buddhi*) when the ultimate goal of the Self has not been reached, and deliverance is nothing but the state in which this aim has been achieved.

The next chapter will explain the psychophysiological techniques through which, according to yoga, this end can be attained. To Samkhya deliverance is obtained almost automatically when the intelligence (*buddhi*) leads man to the threshold of "awakening." Once this self-revelation has been achieved, the intellect, as well as all the other psychomental (and hence material) elements that are incorrectly attributed to the *purusha*, withdraws and is detached from the spirit in order to be reabsorbed in *prakrti*, similar in this respect to a "dancing girl who departs when she has satisfied her master's desire" (this simile is very frequent both in the Mahabharata and in the Samkhya texts; cf. *S.K.*, 59; *S.S.*, III, 69). "There is nothing more sensitive than *prakrti*; as soon as it has said to itself: 'I have been recognized,' it no longer allows itself to be seen by the eyes of the Spirit" (*S.K.*, 61). This is the state of "the man delivered in life" (*jivanmukta*): The wise man goes on living, because he has still his residue of karma to consume (just as the potter's wheel continues to turn because of its acquired momentum even though the pot has already been finished (S.K., 67; S.S., III, 82). But, when in the instant of death he departs from his body, the *purusha* is wholly "delivered" (S.K., 68).

HOW IS DELIVERANCE TO BE ACHIEVED?

In fact both Samkhya and yoga have recognized that "the spirit [*purusha*] can be neither born nor destroyed, that it is neither subjugated nor active [actively striving for deliverance]; that it is neither thirsting for freedom nor delivered" (Gaudapada, *Mandukhya-Karika*, II, 32). "Its way is such that both these possibilities are precluded" (S.S., I, 160). The Self is pure, eternal, free; it would be impossible to subjugate it because it would be incapable of maintaining relations with anything other than itself. But man *believes* that the *purusha* is enslaved and he *thinks* that it can be released. These are illusions of our psychomental life. For in fact the "enslaved" spirit is free through all eternity. If its deliverance seems a struggle to us, it is because we establish ourselves on a human point of view; the spirit is only a "spectator" (*sakshin*), just as "deliverance" (*mukti*) is only a *recognition* of its eternal freedom. *I* think that I am suffering, *I* believe that I am enslaved, *I* desire deliverance. At the moment when I understand—having "awakended"—that this "I" (*asmita*) is a product of matter (*prakrti*), I understand at the same time that the whole of existence has been only a chain of moments of suffering and that the real spirit "impassibly contemplated" the drama of the "personality."

Thus the human personality does not exist as an ultimate element; it is only a synthesis of psychomental experiences, and it is destroyed—that is, it ceases to act—as soon as revelation becomes an accomplished fact. Similar in this respect to all the creations of the cosmic substance, the human personality (*asmita*) too was acting with a view to "awakening"; that is why, once deliverance has been achieved, it becomes useless.

The situation of the spirit (*purusha*), as it is conceived by Samkhya and yoga, is somewhat paradoxical. Although it is pure, eternal, and intangible, the spirit nevertheless consents to its association, even if only illusorily, with matter; and, even in order to take cognizance of its way of being and to be "delivered," it is still compelled to employ an instrument created by *prakrti* (in this instance, intelligence). Undoubtedly, if we consider things from this point of view, human existence seems dramatic to us and indeed devoid of meaning. If the spirit is free, why are men condemned to suffer in ignorance or struggle for a liberty that they already possess? If the *purusha* is completely pure and static, why does it allow impurity, development, experience, suffering, history? These questions could be multiplied. But Indian philosophy reminds us that the Self must not be judged from a logical or historical point of view—that is, by seeking the causes that have determined the present state of things. Reality must be accepted as it is.

It is no less true that on this point the Samkhya position is difficult to support. Therefore, in order to avoid the paradox of this Self utterly deprived of contact with Nature and yet in spite of itself the author of the human drama, Buddhism has totally eliminated the "soul-spirit" considered as an irreducible unit and has replaced it with the "states of consciousness." Vedanta, on the other hand, concerned to avoid the difficulty arising out of the relations between the spirit and the universe, denies the reality of the universe by regarding it as *maya*, illusion. Samkhya and yoga preferred not to deny the ontological reality of either spirit or substance. Hence Samkhya has been attacked particularly because of this doctrine, as much by Vedanta as by Buddhism.

Vedanta also criticizes the conception of the plurality of "selves" (*purusha*) as this has been formulated by Samkhya and yoga. In actuality, these two *darsanas* assert, there exist as many *purushas* as persons. And each *purusha* is a monad, it is completely isolated; for the Self can have no contact either with the surrounding world (derived from *prakrti*) or with other spirits. The cosmos is populated by these eternal, free, immobile *purushas*, monads among which no communication is possible. According to Vedanta, this conception has no foundation and the plurality of "selves" is an illusion. In any event this is a tragic and paradoxical conception of the spirit, which is thus cut off not only from the world of phenomena but also from the other delivered "selves." Nevertheless, Samkhya and yoga have been compelled to postulate the multiplicity of *purushas*; for, if there had been only a single spirit, salvation would have been an infinitely simpler problem and the first man to be delivered would have necessarily brought about the deliverance of the entire human race. If there had been only one universal spirit, the simultaneous existence of "delivered spirits" and "enslaved spirits" would not have been possible. There is more: Not death nor life nor the diversity of sexes and actions could have coexisted in such case (*S.K.*, 18). The paradox is obvious: This doctrine reduces the infinite variety of phenomena to a single principle, matter (*prakrti*); it ascribes to a single source the derivations of the physical universe, life, and consciousness —and yet it postulates the plurality of spirits even though by their nature these are essentially identical. Thus it unites what seems so different—the physical, the vital, and the mental—and isolates what, especially in India, seems so thoroughly unique and universal: the spirit.

THE MEANING OF DELIVERANCE

Let us look more closely at the concept of deliverance (*moksha*) in the doctrines of Samkhya and yoga. As in the majority of the Indian philosophical schools—with the exception, of course, of those that have been influenced by mystic devotion (*bhakti*)—deliverance is in fact an emancipation from the *idea of evil and suffering*. It is only the comprehension of a situation that already existed but that was concealed by the veils of ignorance. Suffering is annihilated of itself as soon as we understand that it is *external to the spirit*, that it concerns

only the human "personality" (*asmita*). Let us indeed imagine
the life of one who has been "delivered." He will continue to
act because the potentials of earlier existences and also those
of his own existence before "awakening" demand to be actualized and consummated in conformity with the law of
karma (see below). But this activity is no longer *his own;*
it is objective, mechanical, disinterested; in short, it is not
undertaken with a view to its "fruit." When the "delivered
man" acts, he is conscious not that "I act" but that "one acts";
in other words, he does not draw the Self into a psychophysical
process. The force of ignorance having lost its energy, new
nuclei of karma are no longer created. When all the "potentials"
that we have mentioned have been destroyed, deliverance is
perfect. It could be said even that the delivered man does not
"experience" his deliverance, After his "awakening" he acts
with indifference, and, when the final psychic molecule is
detached from him, he realizes a mode of being unknown to
mortals because it is absolute: a kind of Buddhist nirvana.

The "freedom" that the Hindu gains by means of metaphysical knowledge or yoga is nevertheless real and concrete. It
is not true that India has sought deliverance only negatively;
for she strives to achieve deliverance positively. In fact, "the
man delivered in life" can expand his sphere of action as far
as he wishes. He has nothing to fear, for his acts no longer have
any *consequences* for him and therefore they have no *limits.*
Since nothing can any longer enslave him, the "delivered man"
can permit himself everything in any field of activity, for what
acts is no longer *he* as "himself" but a mere impersonal instrument.

As for the soteriological conception of Samkhya, to us it
seems daring. Starting from the initial postulate of every Indian
philosophy, *suffering,* and promising to deliver *man* from suffering, Samkhya and yoga are compelled as their journey continues
to deny suffering as such, *human suffering.* This path, considered from the point of view of salvation, leads nowhere,
since it starts from the axiom that the spirit is absolutely free—

By gathering his hair in a knot on the top of his head, the
ascetic symbolizes renunciation

in other words, unsullied by suffering—and ends in the same axiom, namely that the Self is only illusorily drawn into the drama of existence. The only important term in this equation, *suffering*, is left aside; Samkhya does not *eliminate* human suffering, it *denies it as a reality* by denying that it can maintain a real connection with the Self. Suffering remains because it is a cosmic fact, but it loses its significance. Suffering is eliminated *by ignoring it as suffering*. Granted that this elimination is not empiric (through narcotics or suicide), for from the Indian point of view any empiric solution is illusory because it is itself a force of karma. Even the Samkhya solution casts man out of humanity, for it can be realized only by the destruction of the human personality. The yogic practices proposed by Patanjali have the same objective.

These redemptive solutions may seem "pessimistic" to Western man, for whom the personality in spite of everything remains the pillar of all morality and all mysticism. But what matters most to India is not so much the salvation of the personality as the acquisition of *absolute freedom*. When that freedom cannot be won in the present human condition and the personality is charged with suffering and drama, it becomes clear that it is the human condition and the "personality" that must be sacrificed. This sacrifice, furthermore, is largely compensated for by the conquest of absolute freedom thus made possible.

Obviously one could reply that the sacrifice required is too great for its rewards to be able to offer any attraction whatever. Is not the human condition, the dissolution of which is demanded, man's only claim to nobility in fact and in spite of everything? Samkhya and yoga answer this possible criticism by the Westerner in advance when they declare that, until he has gone beyond the level of the psychomental life, man will be able only to prejudge the transcendental "states" that will be the reward of the disappearance of normal consciousness; any value judgment concerning these "states" is automatically invalidated by the mere fact that he who makes it is defined by his own condition, which is of a wholly different order from that on which the value judgment is supposedly made.

Classical yoga begins where Samkhya ends. Patanjali took over the Samkhya philosophy almost totally, but he did not believe that metaphysical knowledge by itself could lead man to liberation. Knowledge, in fact, only prepared the ground with a view to the acquisition of freedom (*mukti*). Emancipation ought, so to speak, to be won through intense struggle, particularly by means of an ascetic technique and a method of contemplation. The objective of yoga, like that of Samkhya, is to abolish normal consciousness for the benefit of a qualitatively different consciousness that can thoroughly understand metaphysical truth. Now for yoga the abolition of normal consciousness is not so easily to be accomplished. In addition to the philosophy, the *darsana*, it also entails a "method" (*abhyasa*), an asceticism (*tapas*): in short, a physiological technique.

This was Patanjali's definition of yoga: "the abolition of states of consciousness" (*Y.S.*, I, 2). As a result yogic technique presupposes the experimental knowledge of all the "states" that "work on" a normal, profane, unilluminated "consciousness." But there is no limit to the number of states of consciousness. All of them, however, fall into three categories corresponding respectively to three possibilities of experience: (1) errors and illusions—dreams, hallucinations, errors in perception, confusion, etc.; (2) the totality of normal psychological experiences—everything felt, perceived, or thought by the profane man, who does not practice yoga; (3) the parapsychological experiences incited by yogic technique and accessible, of course, only to the initiate.

In Patanjali's view each of these "classes" (or categories) of experience has a corresponding science or group of sciences by which experience is governed and that recall experience within the assigned limits when it has exceeded them. The theory of knowledge, for example, as well as logic, has the task of preventing sensory errors and conceptual confusions. "Psychology," law, morality have as their object the totality of the "states of consciousness" of a "normal" man, states that at the same time they evaluate and classify. Since, to yoga and Samkhya, every psychological experience is produced by ignorance of the true nature of the Self (purusha), it follows that "normal" psychic facts, although real from a strictly psychological point of view and valid from a logical point of view (not being illusory like dreams or hallucinations), are nevertheless false from the metaphysical point of view. Metaphysics, indeed, recognizes as valid only a third category of "states," especially those that precede enstasis (samadhi) and prepare for deliverance.

The goal of Patanjali's yoga, then, is to abolish the first two categories of experience (born respectively of logical and of metaphysical error) and to replace them with an enstatic, suprasensory, extrarational "experience." Through samadhi one conclusively goes beyond the human condition—which is dramatic, born of suffering and consummated in suffering—and finally wins that total freedom to which the Indian soul so ardently aspires.

Vyasa, commenting on Y.S., I, 1, offers this classification of the modalities of consciousness (or "mental levels," citta bhumi): (1) unstable; (2) confused, obscure; (3) stable and unstable; (4) fixed on a single point; (5) wholly restrained. The first two modalities are common to all men, for, from the Indian point of view, psychomental life is usually confused. The third modality of consciousness is gained by "occasionally and temporarily" fixating the spirit by means of the concentration of attention (in an effort of memory, for example, or on a problem in mathematics, etc.); but it is transitory and is of no value for deliverance (mukti) because it has not been accomplished through yoga. Only the last two of the modalities enumerated above are yogic "states"—that is, brought about by asceticism and meditation.

Obviously this classification of the modalities and the "dispositions" of consciousness was not made with a view to ordinary knowledge. For, in contrast to Samkhya, yoga assumes the task of destroying, one after another, the various groups, kinds, and varieties of "states of consciousness" (*cittavrtti*). Now this destruction cannot be achieved unless one begins by knowing experimentally, as it were, the structure, the origin, and the intensity of what is doomed to destruction.

"Experimental knowledge" in this context means method, technique, practice. Nothing can be gained without action and without the practice of asceticism (*tapas*); this is a leitmotiv of yogic literature. Books II and III of the *Yoga Sutras* are most especially devoted to this yogic activity (purifications, attitudes of the body, respiratory techniques, etc.). That is why yogic practice is indispensable. In fact, it is only after having tested the first results of this technique by experience that one can acquire faith (*sraddha*) in the efficacy of the method (Vyasa, commenting on Y.S., I, 34). Denial of the reality of the yogic experience or criticism of certain of its aspects cannot come from a man to whom first-hand knowledge of the practice is foreign; for the yogic states go beyond the condition that circumscribes us when we criticize them.

Patanjali and an infinite number of yogic and Tantrist teachers after him knew that the *cittavrtti*, the "whirlwinds of consciousness," could not be controlled and finally eliminated unless they were "experimented with" first. In other words, one cannot be delivered from existence (*samsara*) unless one knows life in a concrete way. This is the explanation of the paradoxical teleology of the Creation, which, according to Samkhya and yoga, on the one hand "enchains" the human soul and on the other incites it to deliverance. In truth the human condition, although dramatic, is not at all desperate, because experiences themselves tend to deliver the spirit (notably by engendering disgust with *samsara* and longing for renunciation). There is more: It is only through *experiences* that one acquires freedom. Therefore the gods (*videha*, "disincarnate")—who have no experience because they have no bodies—have a condition of existence inferior to the human condition, and they cannot attain to total deliverance.

THE SUBCONSCIOUS

Analyzing the "psychic individuality," Patanjali discovered five classes, or, rather, five "matrices" that produced psychomental states (*cittavrtti*): ignorance (*avidya*); the notion of individuality (*asmita*, "*persona*"); passion, attachment (*raga*); disgust (*dvesa*); and love of life, the "will to live" (*abhinivesa*) (Y.S., II, 3, and Vyasa's commentary). These are not five separate psychic functions: The psychic organism is a whole, but its behaviors are multiple. All the classes of *vrtti* are "painful" (*klesa*); hence human experience in its essence is painful. Yoga alone makes it possible to suspend the *vrtti* and abolish suffering.

Thus the yogi must "manipulate" and "manage" these *vrtti* that constitute the psychomental stream. Their ontological cause, of course, is ignorance (Y.S., I, 8). But, in contrast to Samkhya, yoga declares that the mere abolition of metaphysical ignorance is not sufficient to bring about the total destruction of states of consciousness. The reason is that, even though the present "whirlwinds" are eliminated, others would immediately arise to take their place, emerging from the huge reserves of latencies entombed in the subconscious. The concept of *vasana*, which designates these latencies, is of prime importance in yogic psychology; in Patanjali's text it has the meaning of "specific subconscious sensations." The obstacles that these subliminal forces erect on the road that leads to liberation are of two kinds: On the one side the *vasanas* unceasingly feed the psychomental stream, the infinite series of the *cittavrtti*; on the other, and indeed by reason of their specific modalities (subliminal, "germinal"), the *vasanas* form an enormous barrier: for they are imperceptible, difficult to control and dominate. Precisely because their ontological status is that of "potentiality," their own dynamism compels the *vasanas* to manifest themselves, to

The cosmic dance of Siva, surrounded by a halo of flames, trampling a living being, symbolizes mastery through destruction and liberation

"actualize" themselves in the form of acts of consciousness. Thus—even if he has behind him a long practice and has covered many stages of his ascetic journey—the yogi is in danger of being overwhelmed by the invasion of a powerful torrent of psychomental "whirlwinds" precipitated by the *vasanas*.

"The *vasanas* have their origin in the memory," Vyasa said in his commentary on *Y.S.*, IV, 9, thus emphasizing their subliminal character. Life is a constant discharge of *vasanas* that manifest themselves through the *vrtti*. In psychological terms, human existence is an unbroken actualization of the subconscious through the medium of experiences. The *vasanas* condition the specific character of every individual; and this conditioning conforms as much to his heredity as to his karma. In fact, everything that determines the individual's untransmissible specificity, as well as the structure of the human instincts, is produced by the *vasanas*, by the subconscious. This is transmitted either in an "impersonal" fashion, from generation to generation (through language, customs, culture—ethnic and historical transmission), or directly (through karmic transmigration; let us recall the observation that the karmic potentials are transmitted through a "spiritual body," *linga*, literally "rarefied body"). A large part of human experience is the result of this racial and intellectual heritage, those forms of action and thought created by the play of the *vasanas*. These subconscious forces determine the lives of the majority of men. It is only through yoga that they can be known, controlled, and "burned out."

What is characteristic of the human consciousness—as well as of the cosmos in its totality—is the uninterrupted circuit that is established among the various biomental levels. Man's actions (karma), stimulated by the psychomental states (*cittavrtti*), in turn arouse, in fact, other *cittavrtti*. But these states of consciousness are themselves the results of the actualization of the subliminal latencies, the *vasanas*. Thus the latency-consciousness-act-latency-etc. circuit (*vasana-vrtti-karma-vasana-etc.*) offers no solution of continuity. And, since they are manifestations of cosmic matter (*prakrti*), all these modalities of the "psychic substance" are real, and, as such, they would not be susceptible of destruction through a simple act of knowledge (as, in the classic example of Indian philosophy, the illusion of standing face to face with a serpent is "destroyed" when on closer examination one finds that the "serpent" is in reality a stick). The combustion of these subliminal states, of which yoga speaks, means in fact that the Self (*purusha*) detaches itself from the flux of cosmic life. In this case mental energy—which, being determined by the law of karma and projected by igno-rance, was thus far occupying and obscuring the horizon of consciousness—emerges (it too) from the "individual" orbit within which it had moved (*asmita*, personality) and, left to itself, is in the end reincorporated into *prakrti*, the primordial matrix. Man's liberation at the same time "liberates" a fragment of matter by allowing it to return to the primordial unity from which it had come. The "circuit of psychic matter" is closed through yogic technique. In this sense it may be said that the yogi contributes directly and personally to the repose of matter, to the abolition of at least a fragment of the cosmos.

The part played by the subconscious (*vasana*) is important in yogic psychology and technique, for it is the subconscious that conditions not only man's present experience but also his inborn predispositions, as well as his voluntary decisions in the future. Hence it becomes useless to seek to modify the states of consciousness (*cittavrtti*) before the psychomental latencies (*vasanas*) have also been controlled and dominated. If the "destruction" of the *cittavrtti* is to be successful, it is indispen-sable that the subconscious-conscious circuit be broken. This is what yoga attempts to do by putting to work a complex of techniques all of which together are directed to the goal of annihilating the psychomental flux and furthering its "cessa-tion."

Before taking up these various techniques, let us point out

in passing the depth of the psychological analyses made by
Patanjali and his commentators. Long before psychoanalysis,
yoga had shown the importance of the part played by the subconscious. It was indeed in the dynamism peculiar to the
subconscious that yoga saw the most serious obstacle to be
surmounted by the yogi. The reason is that the latencies *want*
to emerge into broad daylight, to become states of consciousness
by being actualized. The resistance that the subconscious offers
against any act of renunciation and asceticism, every action the
effect of which might be the emancipation of the Self, is as it
were the sign of the fear that the subconscious feels at the
mere idea that the mass of yet unmanifested latencies might be
deprived of its destiny, annihilated before it had had time to
manifest and actualize itself.

We were speaking of the resemblance between yoga and
psychoanalysis. In fact, a comparison might well be made, with
a few reservations, all of which, however, are in favor of yoga.
In contrast to Freudian psychoanalysis, yoga does not see only
the libido in the subconscious. Indeed, it brings to light the
circuit that links the subconscious and the conscious, and this
leads it to regard the subconscious as at once matrix and
recipient of all the actions, movements, and intentions of the
ego—in other words, dominated by the "thirst for the fruit"
(*phalatrsna*), the desire for self-satisfaction, for satiety, for
multiplication. It is from the subconscious that *everything that
seeks to manifest itself*—in other words, to assume a "form,"
to demonstrate its "power," to make clear its "individuality"—
comes and it is to the subconscious (thanks to the karmic
"sowings") that it returns.

Again in contrast to psychoanalysis, yoga believes that the
subconscious can be dominated by asceticism, even conquered
by it, through the technique of unifying the states of consciousness, which we shall soon examine. The psychological and parapsychological experience of the East in general and of yoga in
particular is unchallengeably more extensive and more organized

than the experience on which the Western theories of the structure of the psyche have been erected, and so it is probable that on this point too yoga is right and that the subconscious—however paradoxical this may appear to be—can be known, dominated, and conquered.

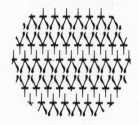

The Techniques of Yoga

CONCENTRATION ON A SINGLE OBJECT

The point of departure for yogic meditation is concentration on a single object, *ekagrata*. This object can be anything—something physical (the point between the eyebrows, the tip of the nose, a luminous object, etc.), a thought (a metaphysical truth), or God (Isvara). The immediate consequence of *ekagrata* is to censure all the psychomental automatisms that dominate and, to be honest, *constitute* profane consciousness. The activities of the senses and the unconscious constantly introduce into consciousness objects that dominate and modify it. Associations diffuse consciousness, passions do it violence. Even in his intellectual efforts man is passive; most of the time he does not

A Sivan ascetic practicing concentration on the point between his eyebrows *think*, properly speaking, but he *allows himself to be thought* by objects. The appearance of thought in reality hides an indefinite, disordered flux, fed by sensations, associations, and memory. The first duty of the yogi is to think: not to allow himself to be thought by objects. That is why yogic practice begins with *ekagrata*, which dams the mental stream and constitutes a "psychic block," a firm, unitary *continuum*.

The practice of *ekagrata* is the endeavor to control the two generative sources of mental fluidity: sensory activity (*indriya*) and subconscious activity (*samskara*). A yogi should be able at will to produce the discontinuity of consciousness: in other words, he can produce, no matter when or where, the concentration of his attention on a "single point" and become insensible to any other sensory or mnemonic stimulus. Through *ekagrata* one acquires a true will—that is, the ability to control freely an important sector of psychosomatic activity.

It follows logically that *ekagrata* can be achieved only through the activation of many exercises and techniques in which physiology plays a major part. It would be impossible, for example, to achieve *ekagrata* if the body was in a tiring position or merely uncomfortable, or if the respiration was disorganized and unrhythmic. That is why yogic technique entails many categories of physiological practices and spiritual exercises (called *anga*, "members"), which one should have learned if one wishes to attain *ekagrata* and, at the extreme, *samadhi*, the supreme concentration. These "members" of yoga can be regarded at the same time as constituting a group of techniques and as representing stages in the spiritual ascetic itinerary whose final stage is definitive liberation. They are: (1) restraints (*yama*); (2) disciplines (*niyama*); (3) the attitudes and positions of the body (*asana*); (4) respiratory rhythm (*pranayama*); (5) the emancipation of sensory activity from the mastery of external objects (*pratyahara*); (6) concentration (*dharana*); (7) yogic meditation (*dhyana*); (8) *samadhi* (Y.S., II, 29).

RESTRAINTS AND DISCIPLINES

The first two groups of practices, *yama* and *niyama*, constitute the inescapable preliminaries for any asceticism. Hence they evidence no specifically yogic peculiarity. There are five "restraints" (*yama*): *ahimsa*, "do not kill"; *satya*, "do not lie"; *asteya*, "do not steal"; *brahmacariya*, "sexual abstinence"; *aparigraha*, "do not be greedy" (Y.S., II, 30).

The "restraints" produce not a yogic state but a "purified" human being, superior to the ordinary run. This purity is essential to the succeeding stages. The purpose of sexual abstinence is the conservation of nervous energy. Yoga ascribes major importance to "the secret forces of the generative faculty," the expenditure of which dissipates the most precious energy, weakens cerebral capacity, and makes concentration difficult. It must be added, however, that sexual abstinence (*brahmacariya*) means not only abstaining from sexual acts but also "burning out" carnal temptation itself.

Side by side with these restraints the yogi must practice the *niyama*—that is, a series of physical and psychic "disciplines." Patanjali declared in Y.S., II, 32, that "cleanliness, serenity, asceticism [*tapas*], the study of yogic metaphysics, and the endeavor to make God [Isvara] the motivation for every action constitute the disciplines." *Cleanliness* means the internal purification of the organs (this is achieved through a series of artificial "purges," on which Hathayoga particularly insists). Vyasa specifies that this purification also implies the expulsion of impurities from the spirit. "The absence of the desire to increase the necessities of existence" is the definition of *serenity*. "*Tapas* [asceticism] consists in enduring opposites, as, for example, the desire to eat and the desire to drink, hot and cold, etc. Study is the knowledge of the sciences relating to deliverance [*moksha*] or the repetition of the syllable OM, etc." (Vyasa, commenting on Y.S., II, 32).

Obviously difficulties arise, even during these exercises, and

Badha-Padmasana

most of them are produced by the dynamisms of the unconscious. The perplexity created by doubt is the most dangerous. Patanjali recommends for its domination the *implantation of the opposite thought* (Y.S., II, 33). It is interesting to note at this point that the yogi's battle against any "obstacle" whatever has a magic character. Every temptation that he overcomes is tantamount to a force that he makes his own. To renounce a temptation is not only to "purify" himself in the negative meaning of this word; it is also to realize a genuine, positive gain: Thus the yogi extends his power over what he had begun by renouncing. And more. He succeeds in *dominating* not only the objects that he had renounced but also a magic force infinitely more precious than all these objects. For example, he who accomplishes the restraint of *asteya* (not stealing) "sees all jewels coming near to him" (Y.S., II, 37). We shall have occasion to come back to these "marvelous powers" (*siddhi*) that the yogi acquires through his discipline.

THE YOGIC ATTITUDES

It is only with the practice of *asana* that yogic technique properly so-called begins. *Asana* designates the well-known yogic posture that the *Yoga Sutras* (II, 46) define as "stable and pleasant." The Hathayoga treatises contain the descriptions of innumerable *asanas*. These descriptions are only sketched in the *Yoga Sutras* because *asana* is learned from a *guru* and not through description. What is important is the fact that *asana* gives a rigid stability to the body while at the same time it reduces physical effort to the minimum. Thus one avoids the irritating sensation of fatigue or of the numbness of certain parts of the body, one controls the physiological processes, and thus one makes it possible for one's attention to be occupied exclusively with the fluid part of consciousness.

In the beginning *asana* is uncomfortable and even intolerable. But, after a certain training period, the effort of keeping the body in the same position becomes minimal. Now this is of

Simple *padmasana* (*asana* of the lotus)

Padangushtasana
(*asana* on the ball of the foot)

Virasana (*asana* of the hero)

Yogamudra (the seal of yoga)

major importance: Effort should disappear and the meditative position should become natural; it is only then that it facilitates concentration. "The posture becomes perfect," Vyasa commented on Y.S., II, 47, "when the effort of achieving it vanishes so that there is no longer any movement in the body." And Vacaspati Misra, commenting on Vyasa's interpretation, said: "He who practices *asana* will have to apply an effort that consists in eliminating the natural bodily efforts. Otherwise the ascetic attitude that is under discussion here cannot be realized."

Asana is one of the characteristic techniques of Indian asceticism. It is found in the Upanishads and even in the Vedic literature, but allusions to it are more abundant in the Epic and in the Puranas. It is in the Hathayogic literature, obviously, that the *asanas* play an increasingly important part; thirty-two varieties are described in the treatise entitled *Gheranda-Samhita*. Here, for instance, is how one achieves one of the easiest and most common meditative positions, *padmasana*: "Place the right foot on the left thigh and, similarly, the left foot on the right thigh; cross the hands behind the back and grip the ends of the feet (the right hand on the right foot and the left hand on the left foot). Rest the chin on the chest and focus the eyes on the tip of the nose" (*Gheranda-Samhita*, II, 8).

There are lists and descriptions of *asanas* in most of the Tantrist and Hathayogic treatises. The purpose of these meditative positions is always the same: "the absolute cessation of agitation by opposites" (Y.S., II, 48). Thus one arrives at a certain "neutrality" of the senses; consciousness is no longer troubled by the "presence of the body." One accomplishes the first stage toward the isolation of consciousness; the bridges that make communication possible with sensory activity begin to be raised.

Asana is the first concrete step taken with a view to the abolition of the modalities of human existence. At the level of the body, *asana* is an *ekagrata*, a concentration on a single point; the body is "concentrated" in a single position. Just as *ekagrata* puts an end to the dispersion and the fluctuations of "states of consciousness," so *asana* puts an end to the mobility and the disposability of the body by infinitely reducing the positions possible in a single, immobile, hieratic attitude. We shall soon see that the tendency toward "unification" and "totalization" is peculiar to all the yogic techniques. But their immediate goal is now at once apparent: It is the abolition (or the transcendence) of the human condition produced by the refusal to conform to the most elementary human inclinations. The refusal to stir, to move (*asana*) will be continued through a whole series of "refusals" of all kinds.

RESPIRATORY DISCIPLINE

Pranayama, the breathing discipline, is the "refusal" to breathe like the general run of men—that is, in an unrhythmic fashion. Here is how Patanjali defines this refusal: "*Pranayama* is the cessation [*viccheda*] of the inhaling and exhaling movements, and it is achieved after *asana* has been mastered" (Y.S., II, 49). Patanjali speaks of "cessation," the suspension of respiration. But *pranayama* begins by enforcing as slow as possible a rhythm on the respiration; and this is its initial objective.

The layman's respiration is usually unrhythmic; it varies either with circumstances or with psychomental tension. This irregularity creates a dangerous psychic fluidity and, consequently, instability and diffusion of attention. One can become attentive by making the effort. But effort, to yoga, is an "externalization." Therefore one attempts by means of *pranayama* to eliminate respiratory effort; cadencing the breathing should become an automatic matter in order that the yogi may forget it.

Bhoja, commenting on the *Yoga Sutras*, I, 34, observed that "there is always a connection between respiration and mental states." This observation is important. It is much more than the verification of the fact that, for example, the respiration of an enraged man is agitated whereas that of a man in concentration is slowed and given rhythm by itself. The relation that connects the rhythm of respiration with the states of consciousness to

Practicing respiratory discipline (*pranayama*) at the start of the *asana* exercises

which Bhoja referred and that had undoubtedly been observed and tested experimentally by yogis since the most ancient times served them as the instrument for the "unification" of the consciousness. The "unification" that is meant here should be construed in this sense that, by progressively retarding his breathing and giving it a rhythm, the yogi can "penetrate"—that is, experience experimentally and with a completely clear mind —certain states of consciousness that are inaccessible when he is in a waking state, particularly those states of consciousness that are characteristic of sleep. The respiratory rhythm of a sleeping man is slower than that of a man awake. By achieving this sleep rhythm by means of *pranayama*, the yogi can penetrate the "states of consciousness" peculiar to sleep without in any way sacrificing his lucidity.

Indian psychology recognizes four modalities of consciousness: waking consciousness, sleeping consciousness with dreams, sleeping consciousness without dreams, and "cataleptic consciousness," *turiya*. Each of these modalities of consciousness is in relation with a specific respiratory rhythm. Through the medium of *pranayama*—that is, by increasingly prolonging inhalation and exhalation—since the purpose of this practice is to allow as long an interval as possible to elapse between these two phases of respiration, the yogi can thus penetrate all the modalities of consciousness. For ordinary persons there is a discontinuity among these various modalities: One goes from the waking to the sleeping state in an unconscious fashion. The yogi should preserve the continuity of consciousness: penetrate each of these states with vigor and lucidity. There is an imposing number of books on this Indian ascetic technique; but most of them merely repeat the traditional recipes. Although *pranayama* is a specific yogic exercise of great importance, Patanjali gave only three sutras to it. Technical details are to be found in the commentaries of Vyasa, Bhoja, and Vacaspati Misra, but principally in the Hathayogic treatises.

The respiratory rhythm is achieved through the harmonization of three "moments": inhalation (*puraka*), exhalation (*re-*

caka), and the retention of the air (*kumbhaka*). Practice enables the yogi to prolong each of these moments for some time. As Patanjali asserted, the purpose of *pranayama* is as long a suspension of respiration as possible, which is arrived at by progressively retarding the rhythm. One begins by holding one's breath for sixteen and a half seconds, then for thirty-three seconds, then for fifty seconds, for three minutes, for five minutes, etc.

BURIED ALIVE

In March 1829 *The Asiatic Monthly Journal* recounted the exploits of a yogi who, among other feats, could remain several hours under water. He refused to explain how he succeeded in doing this, "confining himself to saying that it was a habit with him."

It seems beyond doubt that cataleptic states can be voluntarily brought on by experienced yogis. Doctor Thérèse Brosse has shown that the reduction of respiration and of cardiac contraction to an extent that is generally observable only at the brink of death is an authentic physiological phenomenon that yogis can produce by an effort of will and not at all through the effects of autosuggestion. It goes without saying that such a yogi can be buried alive without danger.

The restriction of respiration [Doctor J. Filliozat wrote] is sometimes such that certain yogis can have themselves buried alive without harm for a specified time, with a cubic volume of air that would be completely inadequate to assure their survival. According to them, this small reserve of air is intended, in the event that some accident should cause them to come out of their yogic state during the experiment and expose them to danger, to supply a few inhalations that would enable them to return to that state [*Magie et Médecine*, Paris, 1943, pp. 115–116].

Let us point out at once that the purpose of these practices is not the acquisition of fakir's powers. We must distinguish

Garbhasana (*asana* of the *fetus*)

between the exhibitionism of certain fakirs and Hathayogis
and the objective pursued by genuine yogis. The latter strive to
dominate their bodies in order to penetrate the secret of psychosomatic life. They want to know experimentally the deep
levels of the psyche and understand their dynamism in order
to find the means of delivering themselves from their domination. Let us not forget that the yogi's ulimate goal is absolute
freedom, perfect autonomy, and this entails a long, complex
labor of conditioning.

CONTROL OF THE BREATH IN CHINA AND ISLAM

The rhythmization and control of the breathing also play an
important part in Taoist techniques (cf. H. Maspéro, *Les procédés de "nourrir le principe vital" dans la religion taoïste
ancienne* in *Journal asiatique*, 1937, pp. 177–252 and 353–430).
The practice was known as "embryonic respiration" (*t'ai-si*)
and its major purpose was to obtain long life (*tch'ang chen*),
which the Taoists construe to be "like a material immortality
of the body itself." Hence "embryonic respiration" is not, like
pranayama, an exercise preliminary to meditation or an auxiliary
exercise. On the contrary, it is sufficient unto itself. Unlike
pranayama, "embryonic respiration" does not serve to prepare
for spiritual concentration, but it does accomplish a process of
"mystic physiology" as a result of which the body's life is in-
definitely prolonged. In this respect Taoism is reminiscent of
Hathayoga, which to a certain extent it resembles. What concerns China above all is the indefinite prolongation of the
physical body's life, whereas what obsesses India is the idea of
the spiritual freedom to be gained, the transfiguration, the
"deification" of the body.

The Taoists practiced holding their breath. They began by
holding it during the period of three, five, seven, nine, twelve
normal respirations, and they claimed that it was possible to

hold it for the time of one hundred twenty respirations or even more. In order to obtain immortality it was necessary to hold one's breath through the period of a thousand normal respirations. But the technique of "internal" or "embryonic" breathing was still more difficult. This was a matter of "dissolving the breath" and making it circulate through the interior of the body. "The supreme purpose is to establish a kind of *internal circulation* of the vital principles such that the individual could remain *completely airtight* and undergo the ordeal of immersion without harm. One becomes *impermeable,* autonomous, invulnerable, once one possesses the art of feeding oneself and breathing in a closed circuit, in the manner of an embryo" (Marcel Granet, *La pensée chinoise,* 1934, pp. 514–515).

It is probable that, at least in its neo-Taoist form, the respiratory discipline has been influenced by Tantrist Yoga: certain practices, at once respiratory and sexual, had reached China as early as the seventh century A.D. (cf. Eliade, *Le Yoga,* p. 395). In addition, China already possessed certain archaic techniques, of Shaman structure, which sought to imitate the movements and breathing of animals. In any event, Lao Tse (*Tao Te King,* 6) and Chuang Tse (Chapter 15) already knew "methodical breathing," and an inscription of the Chu Era attests to the practice of a respiratory technique in the sixth century B.C. (cf. H. Wilhelm, *Eine Chou-Inschrift über Atemtechnik,* in *Monumenta Serica,* XVIII, 1948, pp. 385–388).

Control of the breathing is also practiced by the Moslem mystics. Whatever the *origin* of this technique within the Moslem tradition, it is beyond doubt that certain Moslem mystics in India had borrowed and practiced the yogic exercises. The technique of the *dhikr* sometimes affords striking formal analogies with the Indian respiratory discipline. T. P. Hughes (*A Dictionary of Islam,* London, 1885, pp. 703 ff.) mentions that it was reported of a religious living on the Afghan border that he had so thoroughly practiced the *dhikr* that he succeeded in holding his breath for almost three hours.

HESYCHASM

Certain ascetic preliminaries and methods of prayer employed
by the Hesychast monks show points of resemblance with the
yogic techniques, especially with *pranayama*. Here is Father
Irénée Hausherr's summary of the essence of the hesychast
method of prayer:

It includes a double exercise, omphaloscopy [concentration of vision
on the navel] and the infinite repetition of the prayer to Jesus:
"Lord Jesus Christ, son of God, have pity on me!" Sit in darkness,
bow the head, focus the eyes on the center of the belly, otherwise
called the navel, seek to find the heart's place there, repeat this
exercise without respite, always accompanying it with the same
prayer in accord with the rhythm of the breathing, retarded as
much as possible, and, by dint of persevering day and night in
this mental orison, one will end by finding what one is seeking, the
heart's place, and with it and in it all kinds of marvels and knowledge [Irénée Hausherr, S.J., *La Méthode d'oraison hésychaste*, in
Orientalia Christiana, Volume IX, 2, Rome, 1927, p. 102].

Here is a fragment from Nicophoros the Solitary (second
half of the thirteenth century), recently translated by Jean
Gouillard (*Petite Philocalie de la prière du coeur*, Paris, 1953,
p. 204):

As for you, as I have told you, sit down, collect your spirit, introduce it—I mean your spirit—into your nostrils; this is the route
taken by the breath in order to reach the heart. Push it, force it to
descend into your heart at the same time as the air that you
breathe. When it is there, you will see the joy that will follow:
you will have nothing to regret. As a man who returns to his home
after a long absence can no longer contain his joy at being reunited
with his wife and children, so the spirit, when it is united with
the soul, overflows with unspeakable joy and rapture. My brother,
accustom your spirit then to be in no haste to depart from there.

In the beginning it will be lacking in zeal, that is the least that can be said of this inner reclusion and enclosure. But, once it has acquired this habit, it will no longer find any pleasure in the outside circuits. For "the kingdom of God is within us" and to him who turns his eyes toward it and pursues it with pure prayer all the outer world becomes vile and despicable."

In the eighteenth century the hesychast doctrines and techniques were still familiar to the monks of Mount Athos. Here are a few fragments from the *Encheiridion* of Nicodemus the Hagiorite:

Why the breath must be held during prayer. Inasmuch as her spirit or the act of her spirit has been accustomed from her youth to expand and diffuse itself over the perceptible things of the outer world, for this reason, when she says this prayer, let her not breathe regularly as nature has inured her to doing but let her hold her breath a little until the inner voice has said the prayer through once, and let her then breathe as the divine Fathers have taught her. For through this momentary restriction of respiration the heart is hampered and gripped and consequently it feels pain because it does not receive the air that its nature requires; and the spirit, for its part, collects itself more easily and returns to the heart. . . . For through this momentary restriction of the breath the hard, dense heart is thinned and its fluid, having been suitably compressed and warmed, thus becomes softer, sensitive, humble, and better disposed to compunction and to the easy shedding of tears. . . . For this brief constraint enables the heart to feel tension and pain, and through this tension and this pain it regurgitates the poisoned bait of pleasure and sin that it has earlier swallowed . . . [Hausherr, *op. cit.*, p. 109].

And one must also quote the basic text, *The Method of Holy Prayer and Concentration,* which was long attributed to Simeon the New Theologian. "This little work could well have been contemporary with that of Nicophoros, if it was not written

Posture and respiration in Hesychastic prayer (from a twelfth-century Greek manuscript)

by Nicophoros himself, as I. Hausherr not implausibly speculates" (Gouillard, *op. cit.*, p. 206). I shall use Jean Gouillard's new translation (*Petite Philocalie*, p. 216):

Now sit in a quiet cell, withdrawn into a corner, and concentrate on doing what I tell you: Close the door, elevate your spirit above every vain or transitory object. Then, letting your beard rest on your chest, turn the physical eye as well as the whole spirit toward the center of your belly—that is, toward your navel—compress the inhalation of air that goes through your nose in such fashion as not to breathe easily, and mentally examine the interior of your entrails in search of the heart's place, there where all the powers of the soul love to gather. In the beginning you will find shadows and a stubborn opacity, but, if you persevere, if you practice this exercise night and day, you will find—O marvel!—a felicity without limit.

One must not allow oneself to be deceived by these external analogies with *pranayama*. Among the Hesychasts the purpose of the respiratory discipline and the position of the body was to prepare for mental prayer; in the *Yoga Sutras* these exercises are in furtherance of the "unification" of consciousness and are a preparation for "meditation," and the part played by God (Isvara) is quite small. But it is nonetheless true that the two techniques that we have described are sufficiently similar phenomenologically to justify the consideration of the problem of some influence of Indian mystic physiology on Hesychasm.

THE "WITHDRAWAL OF THE SENSES"

Asana, pranayama, and *ekagrata* have achieved the suspension of the human condition, even if only for the brief interval during which the exercise lasts. Motionless, cadencing his respiration, fixing his eyes and his attention on a single point, the yogi experimentally steps outside the profane modality of existence. He begins to become autonomous in relation to the cosmos; he is no longer troubled by outer tensions (having in

Immobility and concentration, yesterday and today

fact gone beyond "opposites," he is equally insensitive to heat and to cold, to light and to darkness, etc.); sensory activity no longer projects him outward toward the objects of the senses; the psychomental stream is no longer governed by distractions, automatisms, and memory: He is "concentrated," "unified." This withdrawal beyond the cosmos is accompanied by a plunge into the depths of himself. The yogi returns to himself, takes possession of himself, so to speak, surrounds himself with increasingly powerful "defenses"—in a word, he becomes invulnerable.

Asana and *ekagrata* emulate a divine archetype; the yogic position has a religious value in itself. Isvara, the God of the *Yoga Sutras,* is a pure spirit that not only has not created the world but does not even intervene in history, either directly or indirectly. The yogi emulates the way of being that is peculiar to this pure spirit. The transcendence of the human condition, "deliverance," the total autonomy of the *purusha*—the exemplary model for all this is Isvara. Renunciation of the human condition—in other words, the practice of yoga—has a religious value in the sense that the yogi emulates Isvara's way of being: immobility, concentration on himself.

The act of setting a rhythm for respiration and suspending it to the maximum greatly facilitates concentration (*dharana*). For, Patanjali tells us (Y.S., II, 52, 53), as a result of *pranayama,* the veil of the shadows is rent and the intellect becomes capable of concentration (*dharana*). The yogi can verify the quality of his concentration through *pratyahara,* a term that is usually translated as "withdrawal of the senses" or "abstraction" but that I prefer to translate as "faculty of delivering sensory activity from the control of external objects." According to the *Yoga Sutras* (II, 54), *pratyahara* might be interpreted as the faculty by which the intellect (*citta*) has sensations *as if* there were real contact.

Discussing this sutra, Bhoja said that the senses, instead of being directed toward the object, "remain within themselves." Although the senses are no longer attuned to external objects and their activity ceases, the intellect (*citta*) nonetheless does not lose its capacity to have sensory representations. When the *citta* wishes to know an external object, it does not employ a sensory activity; it can know this object through the powers at its disposal. Having been gained directly by contemplation, this "knowledge," from the yogic point of view, is more effective than normal knowledge. "So the yogi's wisdom [*prajna*]," Vyasa wrote, "knows all things as they are" (*Yoga Bhashya*, II, 45).

This emancipation of sensory activity from domination by external objects (*pratyahara*) is the ultimate stage of psycho-physiological asceticism. Henceforth the yogi will no longer be "distracted" or "troubled" by the senses, by sensory activity, by memory, etc. All activity is suspended. The *citta*—since it is the psychic mass that orders and illuminates sensations coming from without—can serve as a mirror of objects without the interposition of the senses between it and its object. The layman is incapable of achieving this freedom because his spirit, instead of being stable, is, on the contrary, unceasingly mauled by the activity of the senses, by the subconscious, and by the "thirst to live." By achieving *cittavrtti nirodhah* (that is, the elimination of psychomental states), the *citta* remains within itself (svarupamatre). But this "autonomy" of the intellect does not entail the elimination of "phenomena." Even though he is detached from phenomena, the yogi continues to contemplate them. Instead of knowing, as he had done heretofore, through the medium of forms (*rupa*) and mental states (*cittavrtti*), the yogi directly contemplates the essence (*tattva*) of all objects.

DHARANA, YOGIC "CONCENTRATION"

His autonomy with respect to the stimuli of the outer world and the dynamism of the subconscious, an autonomy that he achieves through the intermediary of *pratyahara*, makes it possible for the yogi to test a triple technique, which the texts call *samyama* (literally, "going together," "vehicle"). This word

designates the last stages of yogic technique, the three ultimate
"members of yoga" (*yoganga*), namely: "concentration" (*dharana*), "meditation" properly so-called (*dhyana*), and "stasis"
(*samadhi*). These spiritual exercises can be practiced only after
the completion of sufficient repetitions of all the other physiological exercises, when the yogi has succeeded in completely
dominating his body, his subconscious, and his psychomental
flux. These exercises are described as "subtle" (*antaranga*) in
order to emphasize that they entail no new physiological
technique. They are so similar to one another that the yogi
who embarks on one of them (concentration, for instance)
cannot remain within it without difficulty and indeed is likely
in spite of himself to slip into "meditation" or "enstasis."
This is why these three final yogic exercises are given a name
that applies to all of them: *samyama* (Vacaspati Misra, discussing Vyasa, III, 1).

"Concentration" (*dharana*, from the root *dhr*, "to grip
tightly") is in fact an *ekagrata*, a "fixation on a single point,"
but its content is purely abstract. In other words, *dharana*—and
it is in this way that it is distinguished from *ekagrata*, whose
sole purpose is to halt the psychomental flow and "fixate it
on a single point"—achieves this "fixation" in order to *understand*. Here is Patanjali's definition of it: "fixation of thought
on a single point" (*Y.S.*, II, 1). Vyasa specified that concentration was generally fixated on "the center [*cakra*] of the navel,
in the lotus of the heart, in the light of the head, on the tip
of the nose, on the tip of the tongue, or on any external place
or object" (discussing *Y.S.*, III, 1). Vacaspati Misra added
that *dharana* could not be achieved without the help of an
object on which thought was fixed.

DHYANA, YOGIC "MEDITATION"

In his treatise, *Yoga-sara-samgraha* (published by C. Jha,
pages 43 ff.), Vijnana Bhikshu quoted a passage from the

Isvara Gita according to which the duration of *dharana* extends over the period of twelve *pranayamas*. By prolonging this concentration on a single object twelvefold, one attains to "yogic meditation," *dhyana*. Patanjali defined *dhyana* as "a current of unified thought" (*Y.S.*, III, 2), and Vyasa added this gloss: "continuum of mental effort in order to assimilate the object of meditation, free from any other effort to assimilate other objects." Vijnana Bhikshu (*Yoga-sara-samgraha*, p. 45) explained this process in the following manner: When, at the point to which *dharana* has been practiced, the spirit has succeeded in holding itself before itself in the form of the object of meditation for a sufficient time, without any interruption brought on by the intrusion of some other function, one then arrives at *dhyana*. As an example he offered the contemplation of Vishnu or of some other god whom one imagines to be present in the lotus of one's heart.

It is unnecessary to point out that this yogic "meditation" is completely different from profane meditation. First of all, no mental "continuum" in the framework of normal psychomental experience can acquire the density and the purity to which yogic practices enable us to attain. In the second place, profane meditation is limited either to the outer form of the objects on which one is meditating or to their value, whereas *dhyana* makes it possible to "penetrate" objects, to "assimilate" them magically.

The act of "penetrating" the essence of objects is particularly difficult to explain; it must not be conceived either under the guise of poetic imagination or under that of a Bergsonian type of intuition. What clearly differentiates yogic "meditation" from these two irrational impulses is its coherence, the state of lucidity that accompanies it and that constantly maintains it on course. In actuality the "mental continuum" never eludes the yogi's control. At no time is this continuum laterally enriched by uncontrolled associations, analogies, symbols, etc. At no time does the meditation cease to be an *instrument* of penetration into the essence of things—finally, in other words, an instrument for the *acquisition of possession,* for the "assimilation" of the real.

In contrast to Samkhya, yoga asserts the existence of a deity, Isvara (literally, "the Lord"). This God, of course, is not a creator (since, as we have seen, the cosmos, life, and man were created by *prakrti,* for all come from the primordial substance). But in some men Isvara can accelerate the process of deliverance; he helps them to attain more quickly to *samadhi.* The Lord of whom Patanjali spoke is, rather, a God of yogis. It is only a yogi to whom he can render help—that is, a man who has already chosen yoga. Isvara's function, moreover, is quite modest. For example, he can enable the yogi who takes him as an object of concentration to attain to *samadhi.* According to Patanjali (Y.S., II, 45), this divine succor is the effect not of a "desire" or a "feeling"—for the Lord can have neither desires nor emotions—but of a "metaphysical sympathy" between Isvara and *purusha,* a sympathy that is explained by the congruency of their structures. Isvara is a *purusha* free through all eternity, never tainted by the "sufferings" and "impurities" of existence (Y.S., I, .24). Commenting on this passage, Vyasa pointed out that the difference between the "emancipated spirit" and Isvara was this: The spirit was once (even illusorily) in relation with psychomental experience, while Isvara has always been free. Isvara does not allow himself to be influenced by rituals or devotion or faith in his "grace"; but his "essence" collaborates instinctively, so to speak, with the Self that seeks to emancipate itself through yoga.

Rather is it a sympathy of a metaphysical character that connects two related entities with each other. It might be said that this sympathy that Isvara evidences toward some yogis—that is, toward those few men who seek their deliverance by means of yogic techniques—has drained Isvara of his capacity to take an

Siva as a "great yogi," with the knot of hair, the lunar crescent, and the third eye in the forehead

interest in the fate of human beings. That is why neither
Patanjali nor Vyasa could successfully and precisely explain
God's intervention in Nature. It becomes apparent that Isvara,
as it were, made his way into the dialectic of Samkhya and yoga
from without. In fact, Samkhya asserts (and yoga endorses the
statement) that substance (*prakrti*), through its "teleological instinct," collaborates in man's deliverance. Thus the part that
God plays in the acquisition of this freedom is deprived of importance; cosmic substance assumes the duty of delivering the
many "Selves" (*purushas*) caught in the illusory nets of existence.

Although he had introduced into Samkhya's soteriological
doctrine this new and all things considered completely useless
element of Isvara, nevertheless Patanjali did not grant him the
importance that was to be ascribed to him by future commentators. What is of the first importance in the *Yoga Sutras* is
technique; in other words, the yogi's will and his capacity
for self-domination and concentration. Why nevertheless did
Patanjali find it necessary to introduce Isvara? Because Isvara
corresponded to a reality of an experimental nature: Isvara
could in fact produce *samadhi* provided that the yogi practice
Isvarapranidhana, or devotion to Isvara (*Y.S.*, II, 45). In setting
himself the task of collecting and classifying all the yogic techniques validated by the "classical tradition," Patanjali could not
neglect a whole series of experiences that only concentration on
Isvara could have made possible. In other words, side by side
with the tradition of a purely magical yoga tradition—that is,
calling only on the personal will and strength of the ascetic—
there existed another, "mystic" tradition in which the final
stages of yoga were at least made easier through a devotion—
even if extremely rarefied, extremely "intellectual"—to a God.
At least as he was portrayed by Patanjali and Vyasa, however,
Isvara is deprived both of the greatness of the creative, all-
powerful God and of the pathos proper to the dynamic, solemn
God of the various mysticisms. Isvara, in sum, is merely an
archetype of the yogi: a macroyogi; very probably the patron of

certain yogic sects. In fact Patanjali makes it clear that Isvara has been the *guru* of the sages since time immemorial; for, he adds, Isvara is not bound by time (Y.S., I, 26).

Let us nevertheless emphasize at this point a detail the significance of which will not become clear until later: In a dialectic of deliverance in which it was not required that he appear, Patanjali introduced a "God" to whom, it is true, he ascribed only a quite modest function. For *samadhi*—as we shall see—can be attained even without this "concentration on Isvara." The yoga practiced by Buddha and his contemporaries dispensed with this "concentration on God." It would indeed be very easy to imagine a yoga that would accept the whole of the Samkhya dialectic, and we have no reason to believe that such a magical, atheist yoga did not exist. Patanjali, however, was compelled to introduce Isvara into yoga; for Isvara, so to speak, was an experimental fact: Certain yogis did indeed call on Isvara even though they could have attained to deliverance through the exclusive observance of yogic technique.

Here we are dealing with the magic-mystic polarity so characteristic of medieval Indian spirituality. What is remarkable is the increasingly active part that Isvara was to play for the later commentators. Vacaspati Misra and Vijnana Bhikshu, for example, ascribed great importance to him. It is true that these two commentators interpreted Patanjali and Vyasa in the light of the spirituality of their own later time. But they lived in a period in which the whole of India was saturated with mystic and devotional currents. Yet it is precisely this almost universal triumph of "mysticism" that is most significant when it comes to "classical" yoga, which was thus removed from what had been characteristic of it at its origin: namely, "magic." Thus, under the joint influences of certain Vedantic ideas and *bhakti* (mystical devotion), Vijnana Bhikshu devoted much thought to the "special grace of God" (*Yoga-sara-samgraha*, pp. 9, 18–19, 45–46). Another commentator, Nilakantha, declared that, though inactive, God helped the yogis like a magnet (cf. Dasgupta, *Yoga as Philosophy and Religion*, page 89). The

same author ascribed to Isvara a "will" capable of predestining
men's lives; for "those whom he wishes to raise he goads to
perform good deeds and those whom he wishes to destroy he
goads to commit evil deeds" (*ibid.*, p. 88). How far we have
come from the modest place that Patanjali assigned to Isvara!

ENSTASIS AND HYPNOSIS

It will be remembered that the three "members of yoga"
represent "experiences" and "states" so closely linked to one
another that they have all been given the same name: *samyama*.
Hence to realize *samyama* on a given "plane" means to achieve
simultaneously "concentration" (*dharana*), "meditation" (*dhyana*), and "stasis" (*samadhi*): this "plane," or level, might for
example be that of inert matter (the earth, etc.) or that of
incandescent matter (such as "fire"). The transition from "concentration" to "meditation" requires the utilization of no new
technique. Similarly, no supplementary yogic exercise is required
for the realization of *samadhi* once the yogi has succeeded in
"concentrating" and "meditating." *Samadhi*, yogic "enstasis,"
is the final result, the coronation of all the ascetic's efforts and
spiritual exercises. (The word *samadhi* has all these meanings:
union, totality; absorption in; total concentration of the spirit;
conjunction. It is usually translated as "concentration"; but in
this case there is the risk of confusion with *dharana*. It is for
this reason that I have preferred to translate it as enstasis, stasis,
conjunction.)

There is no limit to the difficulties to be overcome if one
seeks really to understand exactly in what this yogic "stasis" consists. Even if one leaves aside the cognate meanings that the
concept of *samadhi* assumes in Buddhist literature, as well as in
the "baroque" versions of yoga, and even if one restricts oneself
to consideration of the meaning and the value that have been
given to the word by Patanjali and his commentators, the difficulties remain. For, on the one hand, *samadhi* denotes an "experience" that is indescribable from any point of view; on the

Ramakrishna in *samadhi*, supported by one of his disciples

other, this "enstatic experience" is not univalent; its modalities are very many. Let us attempt, proceeding by stages, to see to what *samadhi* refers. The word is used first of all in a gnostic sense: *samadhi* is that contemplative state in which thought immediately grasps the form of the object without the help of categories or imagination (*kalpana*); a state in which the object reveals itself "in itself" (*svarupa*), in what is essential in it, and as if it "were empty of itself" (Y.S., III, 3). Vacaspati Misra, commenting on this passage, quoted another from the Vishnu Purana (VI, 90), which stated that the yogi who has stopped using his "imagination" no longer regards the *act* and the *object* of meditation as distinct from each other. There exists a real coincidence between the *knowledge* of the object and the *object of knowledge;* this object no longer appears to consciousness in the relations that define and delimit it as a phenomenon, but "as if it were empty of itself." Illusion and imagination (*kalpana*) are thus completely eliminated by *samadhi*. Or, as Vijnana Bhikshu put it (*Yoga-sara-samgraha*, p. 44), one arrives at *samadhi* "when *dhyana* is delivered from the separate notions of 'meditation,' 'object of meditation,' and 'meditating subject' and is sustained solely in the form of the object meditated on"—that is, when there no longer exists anything outside this new ontological dimension represented by the transformation of the "object" (the world) into "knowledge-possession." Vijnana Bhikshu added that there was a clear difference between *dhyana* and *samadhi:* Meditation can be interrupted "if people enter into contact with attracting objects," whereas *samadhi* is an invulnerable state completely impervious to stimuli.

This yogic state, however, must not be regarded as a mere hypnotic trance. Indian psychology knows hypnosis and attributes it to a fortuitous, temporary state of concentration (*vikshipta*). Certain episodes of the Mahabharata reveal the popular Indian conception of hypnosis. According to this conception, the hypnotic trance is merely an automatic dam in the "river of consciousness" and not a yogic *ekagrata*. Furthermore, in his treatise entitled *Spanda Karika*, Bhatta Kallata described the differences between the hypnotic or somnambulist trance and *samadhi*. The state called *vikshipta* is only a paralysis of the mental flow, emotional or volitional in its origin; this dam should not be confused with *samadhi*, which is achieved exclusively through *ekagrata*—in other words, after the plurality of mental states has been eliminated (Y.S., III, 11).

SAMADHI "WITH SUPPORT"

But *samadhi* is a "state," an enstatic modality peculiar to yoga, rather than "knowledge." We shall soon see that this "state" makes possible the autorevelation of the Self (*purusha*) thanks to an act that is not a constituent of an "experience." But it is not every *samadhi* that reveals the Self, it is not every "stasis" that makes final deliverance real. Patanjali and his commentators differentiated among many kinds or stages of supreme concentration. When *samadhi* is achieved with the help of an object or a thought (that is, by concentrating thought on a point in space or on an idea), the enstasis is called *samprajnata samadhi* (enstasis "with support," or "differentiated"). When, on the contrary, *samadhi* is attained without any "relation" (whether of external or mental character)—in other words, when one achieves a "conjunction" in which there was no intervention of "otherness," but which is simply a full comprehension of being—it is *asamprajnata samadhi* ("undifferentiated" enstasis) that is accomplished. Vijnana Bhikshu (*Yoga-sara-samgraha*, p. 4) pointed out that *samprajnata samadhi* was a means of deliverance to the extent to which it made possible the comprehension of truth and put a term to every kind of suffering. But *asamprajnata samadhi* destroys the "impressions [*samskara*] of all prior mental functions" and succeeds even in arresting the forces of karma unleashed earlier by the yogi's past activities. During "differentiated enstasis," Vijnana Bhikshu added, all the mental functions are arrested ("inhibited"), with the exception of that function that "meditates on the object,"

Yantra: a diagram intended to concentrate thought
on the idea of the divinity

while in *asamprajnata samadhi* all "consciousness" vanishes:
The whole of the mental functions is blocked. "During this
stasis there exists no other trace of the spirit [*citta*] outside the
impressions [*samskara*] left behind [by its prior operation]. If
these impressions were not there, there would be no possibility
of a return to consciousness."

Hence we are confronted by the existence of two sharply
different classes of "states." The first series is achieved by means
of the yogic technique of concentration (*dharana*) and meditation (*dhyana*); the second class consists in fact in a single
"state": unprovoked enstasis, "rapture." Undoubtedly even this
asamprajnata samadhi is always the result of the yogi's prolonged efforts. It is neither a gift nor a state of grace. It could
hardly be achieved before the kinds of *samadhi* embraced in
the first class had been sufficiently experienced. It is the reward
of the innumerable "concentrations" and "meditations" that

preceded it. But it comes without being sought, without being provoked, without express preparation for it: That is why it can be called a "rapture."

Obviously "differentiated enstasis," *samprajnata samadhi*, consists in a number of stages; this results from the fact that it is perfectible and that it does not achieve an absolute, irreducible "state." As a rule four stages or kinds are identified: "argumentative" (*savitarka*), "non-argumentative" (*nirvitarka*), "reflexive" (*savicara*), and "super-reflexive" (*nirvicara*) (cf. Y.S., I, 42–44). Patanjali knew another terminology as well: *vitarka, vicara, ananda, asmita* (Y.S., I, 17). But, as Vijnana Bhikshu observed, reproducing this second list, "the four terms are purely technical, they are customarily applied to different forms of realization." These four forms or stages of *samprajnata samadhi*, he continued, represent an ascent: Isvara's grace, in certain cases, makes it possible to attain directly to the higher states and then it is unnecessary to go back and achieve the preliminary states. But, when there is no intercession by this divine grace, the four stages must be accomplished in succession with the same object of meditation.

In the first stage, *savitarka* (the "argumentative"—Y.S., I, 42 —because it presupposes a preliminary analysis), thought identifies itself with the object meditated on "in its essential totality"; for an object is composed of a *thing*, an *idea*, and a *word*, and these three "aspects" of its reality are in perfect consonance with thought (*citta*) during meditation. *Savitarka samadhi* is achieved through concentration on objects envisaged in their substantive aspect (*sthula*, "unrefined"): this is a "direct perception" of objects, but it also extends both to their past and to their future. For instance, Vijnana Bhikshu pointed out, if one practices *savitarka samadhi* with relation to Vishnu, one envisages that god in his substantive form and situated in the region of heaven that is rightfully his, but one also perceives him as he was in the past and as he will be in a more or less distant future. This is tantamount to saying that this kind of *samadhi*, even though produced by "coalescence" (*samapatti*) with the "unrefined" aspect of a reality (in this illustration, direct perception of Vishnu's corporeality), nonetheless is not reduced to the immediacy of the object, but also "pursues" and "assimilates" it in its temporal term.

The next stage, *nirvitarka* ("non-argumentative"), was described in these terms by Vyasa (discussing *Y.S.,* I, 43): "*Citta* becomes *nirvitarka* after memory has stopped functioning—that is, after verbal or logical associations have halted; at the moment when the object is barren of name and meaning; when thought is reflected in a direct manner by espousing the form of the object and glows only with that object in itself (*svarupa*)." In this meditation, thought is delivered from the presence of the "ego," for the act of cognition ("I know that object" or "that object is mine") no longer takes place; it is thought that *is* (becomes) that object (Vacaspati Misra, I, 43). The object is no longer known through associations—that is, incorporated into the series of prior representations, localized through extrinsic relations (name, size, use, class), and, so to speak, impoverished through the usual process of abstraction characteristic of profane thought; it is grasped directly, in its existential nakedness, as a concrete, irreducible fact.

"KNOWLEDGE STATES"

Let us note that in these stages *samprajnata samadhi* is shown to be a "state" achieved through a certain "knowledge." Contemplation makes enstasis possible; enstasis, in turn, makes it possible to penetrate more deeply into reality by producing (or facilitating) a new contemplation, a new yogic "state." This passage from "knowledge" to "state" must be kept constantly in mind; for in my view it is the characteristic quality of *samadhi* (as it is, for that matter, of all Indian "meditation"). In *samadhi* there occurs that "fracture of level" that India seeks to achieve and that is the paradoxical transition from *being* to *knowing.* This suprarational "experience," in which the real is dominated and assimilated by knowledge, leads ultimately to

At the *ashram* of Tiruvannamalar, Etche Amma has attained to a high degree of "realization" through the practice of Jnana Yoga

the fusion of all modalities of being. That this is the deepest
meaning and the major function of *samadhi* is what we shall
see somewhat later. What I wish to emphasize for the moment
is that *savitarka samadhi*, like *nirvitarka samadhi*, is a "knowledge state" achieved through concentration and meditation on
the formal unity of "objects."

But one must go beyond these stages if one wishes to penetrate into the very essence of things. This is how the yogi begins
his *savicara* ("reflexive") meditation; thought is no longer arrested at the outer aspect of material objects (objects that are
composed of aggregates of atoms, physical particles, etc.); on
the contrary, it gains direct knowledge of those infinitesimal
nuclei of energy that the Samkhya and yoga texts call *tanmatra*.
One meditates on the "rarefied" aspect (*sukshma*) of matter;
one penetrates, according to Vijnana Bhikshu, to *ahamkara* and
prakrti, but this meditation is still accompanied by awareness of
time and space (not of the "experience" of a given space or a
given time but of the categories of time and space).

When thought "identifies itself" with the *tanmatra* without
experiencing the "feelings" that by their energetic nature these
tanmatra produce—in other words, when the yogi "assimilates
them in the ideal fashion," without the consequence of a feeling
of suffering or pleasure or violence or inertia, etc., and without
being conscious of time and space—one achieves the state of
nirvicata. Thought is now merged with those infinitesimal nuclei
of energy that constitute the authentic foundation of the
physical universe. This is a true plunge into the very essence of
the physical world and not merely into qualified and individ-
uated phenomena (Vyasa and Vacaspati Misra discussed these
stages in their commentaries on Y.S., I, 44, 45).

All these four stages of *samprajnata samadhi* are called
bijasamadhi (*samadhi* with "seed") or *salambana samadhi* (with
"support"); for, Vijnana Bhikshu declared, they are related to
a "substratum" (support) and produce tendencies that are like
"seeds" for the future functions of consciousness (see also
Bhoja on Y.S., I, 17). On the other hand, *asamprajnata samadhi*

A *mahasiddha*, or yogi who has attained to miraculous powers
(eighteenth-century Tibetan painting)

is *nirbija*, "without seed," without "support" (Vyasa on Y.S., I, 2). By proceeding through the four stages of *samprajnata*, one obtains the "faculty of absolute knowledge" (*rtambharaprajna*) (Y.S., I, 48): this is already an approach toward *samadhi* "without seed," for absolute knowledge reveals the ontological pleni- tude in which *being* and *knowledge* are no longer discrete from each other. Fixated in *samadhi*, consciousness (*citta*) can now enjoy the immediate revelation of the Self (*purusha*). By reason of the very fact that this contemplation (which is in actuality a "participation") is achieved, the pain of existence is abolished (Vijnana Bhikshu, *Yoga-sara-samgraha*, p. 5).

"MIRACULOUS POWERS"

It is when he has reached this stage in his meditative dis- cipline that the yogi acquires the "miraculous powers" (*siddhi*) to which Book III of the *Yoga Sutras* is dedicated from sutra 16 on. By "concentrating," by "meditating," by achieving *samadhi* with regard to a specific object or a whole class of objects—in other words, by practicing *samyama*—the yogi ac- quires certain occult "powers" with respect to the object or objects involved in his experiment.

So, for example, by exercising *samyama* with respect to sub- conscious residues (*samskara*), he knows his previous existences (III, 18). Through *samyama* exercised on "ideas" (*pratyaya*), the yogi knows the "mental states" of other men (III, 19). "But this knowledge of mental states does not imply knowledge of the objects that produced them, for these objects are not in direct communication with the yogi's thought. He knows the mental emotion of love but he does not know the object of love" (Vyasa, *ibid.*).

Samyama, it will be remembered, designates the three final "members of yoga": *dharana*, *dhyana*, and *samadhi*. The yogi begins by concentrating on an "object," an "idea"; let us say, for example, his subconscious residues (*samskara*). When he has succeeded in attaining *ekagrata* concerning these residues, he begins to "meditate" them—that is, to assimilate them magically into himself, to appropriate them. *Dhyana*, meditation, makes possible *samprajnata samadhi*, in this instance *bija samadhi*, *samadhi* with support. (In our illustration the supports are obviously the subconscious residues themselves.) Through yogic enstasis achieved on the basis of these residues, one succeeds not only in understanding and magically assimilating these residues (this had already been made possible by *dharana* and *dhyana*) but also in transmuting "knowledge" into "possession." As a consequence *samadhi* uninterruptedly identifies him who meditates with that on which he meditates. It follows naturally that, by understanding these subconscious residues to such a point that he becomes the residues themselves, the yogi knows them not only as residues but also by taking their place in the whole from which they were detached; in sum, he can relive his earlier existences ideally (that is, without "experiencing" them).

To recall the other example (*Y.S.*, III, 19): as a result of *samyama* with respect to "concepts," the yogi realizes the whole of the infinite series of the psychomental states of other men; for, once he has "mastered a concept from within," the yogi sees, as on a screen, all the states of consciousness that this concept is capable of producing in other men's souls. He sees an infinity of situations that this concept can engender, for he has not only assimilated the content of the "concept" into himself but in addition penetrated into his inner dynamism, he has made his own the human destiny possessed by the concept, etc. Some of these powers are even more miraculous. In his list of the *siddhi*, Patanjali mentions all those legendary "powers" by which Indian mythology, folklore, and metaphysics are obsessed with equal intensity. In contrast to the folklore texts, Patanjali offers us some very summary illuminations on them. Thus, seeking to explain why *samyama* with respect to the shape of the body can make him who practices it invisible, Patanjali says that *samyama* makes the body imperceptible to other men and, "no further direct contact with the light of the eyes being possible, the body disappears" (*Y.S.*, III, 20). This

The Madras Brahman who claimed to sit in the air by Yoga powers.

REWARD OF RS. 1,000.

The above sum is offered to any one who, by yoga powers, will raise himself three feet from the ground, and remain suspended for ten minutes. For conditions, see page 38.

A constant feature of folklore: the miracle of the rope, to the end of which the yogi supposedly hoists himself

is Patanjali's explanation for the disappearances and apparitions of yogis, a miracle cited in an infinite number of Indian religious, alchemist, and folklore documents.

Patanjali also mentions the other "powers" that can be acquired through *samyama*, such as that of knowing the instant of death (*Y.S.*, III, 21), or remarkable physical powers (III, 23), or the knowledge of "subtle" things (III, 24), etc. By practicing *samyama* on the plexus of the navel (*nabhicakra*) one acquires the knowledge of the corporeal system (III, 28); by exercising *samyama* on the cavity of the neck (*kanthakupe*), one makes hunger and thirst vanish (III, 29); the practice of *samyama* on the heart gives one the knowledge of the spirit (III, 33). "Whatever the yogi desires to know, he should achieve *samyama* with respect to that object" (Vacaspati Misra on *Y.S.*, III, 30). This "knowledge" acquired through the techniques of *samyama* is in fact a possession, an assimilation of the realities on which the yogi meditates. Everything that is "meditated"—through the magic virtue of meditation—is assimilated, possessed. It is not difficult to understand that the profane have always confused these "powers" (*siddhi*) with yoga's vocation. In India a yogi has always been regarded as a *mahasiddha*, a possessor of occult powers, a "magician." That this uninformed opinion is not wholly mistaken is made clear to us by the whole spiritual history of India, where the magician has always played an important part. India has never been able to forget that in certain circumstances man can become a "man-god." She has never been able to accept the prevailing human condition composed of suffering, powerlessness, and precariousness. She has always believed that there are men-gods, magicians, for she has always had before her the example of the yogis. That all these men-gods and magicians have striven to transcend the human condition is clear from the evidence. But very few of them succeeded in going beyond the condition of the *siddha*, the "magician" or "god." In other words, there have been very few who have succeeded in overcoming the second temptation, that of making a place for oneself in a "divine condition."

Some of the magicians (*mahasiddhas*) of the Tibetan tradition, portrayed surrounding the Sacred Lama (eighteenth-century Tibetan painting)

Buddha himself, before his illumination, was the target of the temptations reserved for the ascetic by the daughters of heaven (seventh-century mural from a grotto at Ajanta)

"COME AND REJOICE HERE IN HEAVEN"

It is in fact known that in India's view renunciation has a positive value. He who renounces feels that by so doing he has been not diminished but, on the contrary, enriched; for the strength that he gains through renouncing any pleasure far exceeds the pleasure that he has renounced. Thanks to renunciation and asceticism (*tapas*), men, demons, or gods can become so powerful as to be dangers to the economy of the entire universe. In myths, legends, and stories there are innumerable episodes in which the chief character is an ascetic—a man or a demon—who, as a result of the magic power that he has obtained through his "renunciation," can trouble the repose of even Brahma or Vishnu. In order to avert such an increase in sacred strength, the gods "tempt" the ascetic. Patanjali himself spoke of the heavenly temptations—those, that is, that come from divine beings (*Y.S.*, III, 51)—and Vyasa offered these explanations: When the yogi attains to the final differentiated enstasis, the gods approach him and urge, by way of temptation: "Come and rejoice here in heaven. These pleasures are desirable, this girl is adorable, this elixir does away with old age and death," etc. They continue tempting him with celestial women, supernatural vision and hearing, the promise of transforming his body into a "body of diamonds"—in a word, they offer to share the divine condition with him (Vyasa on *Y.S.*, III, 51). But the divine condition is still far from absolute freedom. It is the yogi's duty to reject these "magic mirages," these "false sensory objects endowed with the nature of dream," "desirable only to the ignorant," and to persevere in his task: the achievement of final deliverance.

For, as soon as the ascetic agrees to make use of the magic powers acquired through his abstentions, he at once loses any possibility of gaining new powers. He who renounces profane life finds himself in the end rich in magic powers; but he who succumbs to the temptation to use these magic powers is in the end merely a "magician" whose power to transcend himself is

Siva as Dakshinamurti, the god of knowledge. Her meditation belt is still in place on one leg (Conjeevaram, eighth century)

lost. Only a new renunciation and a victorious struggle against
the temptation of magic can bring new spiritual enrichment to
the ascetic. According to Patanjali and the whole tradition of
"classical" yoga—to say nothing of the metaphysics of Vedanta,
which holds all "power" in contempt—the yogi employs the
innumerable *siddhi* with a view to gaining supreme freedom,
asamprajnata samadhi, and not at all to winning domination—
which, for that matter, is only fragmentary and temporary—
over the elements. For it is *samadhi,* and not "occult powers,"
that represents true "domination." In fact, Patanjali tells us
(III, 37), these powers are "perfections" (this is the literal
meaning of *siddhi*) in the waking state, but they constitute
obstacles in the state of *samadhi*—a natural condition if one
recalls that in Indian thought all possession implies subjection
to what is possessed.

And yet the longing for the "divine condition," attained by
main strength, magically, has never ceased to obsess the yogis
and the ascetics. This is all the more the case since, according
to Vyasa (on Y.S., III, 26), there is a great similarity between
certain gods inhabiting the celestial regions (in the Brahmaloka)
and the yogis in the stage of *siddhi*—in other words, possessors
of "perfections" gained through *samprajnata samadhi.* In fact,
Vyasa asserted, the four classes of gods in the Brahmaloka have
by their very nature "spiritual situations" that respectively correspond to the four classes of differentiated *samadhi.* Because
these gods have been arrested at the stage of *samadhi* "with
support" (with "seed"), they have not been delivered: They
enjoy only an exceptional condition, the same situation acquired
by yogis when they become masters of the "perfections."

This gloss by Vyasa is important: It shows us that the yogis
are made the equals of the gods—in other words, that the path
of yoga (through the "magic" and the "religion" that it includes) leads to a mythological perfection, the same perfection
as that of the members of the Indian pantheon. But, just like
the Vedantist who pursues only the knowledge of Absolute
Being (*Brahma*), the true yogi does not allow himself to be

Milarepa, a Tibetan ascetic who achieved the peak of "realization" through the Tantrist Yoga of the Kagyupa sect in the eleventh century (Tibetan painting)

tempted by the divine condition, which, however alluring it may be, is no less "conditioned," and he strives to arrive at the knowledge and possession of the Self: in other words, the final deliverance represented by *asamprajnata samadhi*.

SAMADHI "WITHOUT SUPPORT" AND FINAL DELIVERANCE

There is a constant oscillation among the various degrees of *samprajnata samadhi*, not because of the instability of thought but because of the close, organic bond that exists among the various types of *samadhi* with support. The yogi goes from one to another, his disciplined, purified consciousness exerting itself by turns in various species of contemplation. According to Vyasa (on Y.S., I, 2), at this stage the yogi is still aware of the difference between *citta* merely reduced to its luminous mode of being (*sattva*) and *purusha*. When this difference disappears, he attains *asamprajnata samadhi*; then all *vrtti* is abolished, "consumed"; all that remains are the unconscious impressions (*samskara*) (Y.S., I, 18, with Vyasa's commentary), and at a certain moment even these imperceptible *samskara* are consumed (Y.S., I, 51); then comes the real enstasis "without seed" (*nirbija samadhi*).

Patanjali specified (Y.S., I, 19) that there were two kinds of undifferentiated *samadhi*, or, more precisely, that there were two avenues, two possibilities for its achievement: the technical way (*upaya*) and the natural way (*bhava*). The first is that of the yogis, who conquer *samadhi* by means of yoga; the second is that of the gods (*videha*, "the disincarnate") and of a class of superhuman beings called "those absorbed in *prakrti*" (*prakrtilaya*). Here again we find the homologation of the yogis to gods and superhuman beings that we have just seen in connection with the various stages of *samprajnata samadhi*. Commenting on this sutra of Patanjali, Vyasa and Vacaspati Misra emphasized the superiority of the enstasis achieved by the yogis through their technique (*upaya*), for the "natural" *samadhi* enjoyed by the gods is temporary, even though it endures for thousands of cosmic cycles. Let us note in passing the stress employed to proclaim the superiority of human yoga with respect to the apparently privileged conditions of the gods.

Vijnana Bhikshu looked at the matter somewhat differently (*Yoga-sara-samgraha*, pages 18 ff.). To him *upayapratyaya*, the "artificial" method (in the sense that it is not "natural" but a construction), consists in practicing *samyama* on Isvara and, if one lacks the mystic vocation, on one's own Self: this method is the one usually employed by yogis. As for the second way, the "natural" method, certain yogis can attain to undifferentiated enstasis (and hence to final deliverance) through their mere desire for it; in other words, it is no longer a conquest achieved by technical methods, it is a spontaneous operation. It is called *bhava*, "natural," Vijnana Bhikshu stated, precisely because it results from the birth (*bhava*) of those who obtain it—that is, birth at a propitious moment, thanks to the practice of yoga in an earlier existence. This second avenue, *bhavapratyaya*, is characteristic of the *videha* (beings without bodies), the *prakrtilaya* (those absorbed in *prakrti*), and other divinities. As an example of the *videha*, Vijnana Bhikshu cited Hiranyagarbha and other gods who had no need for physical bodies because they were capable of performing all the physiological functions in "rarefied" bodies. The *prakrtilayas* were superhuman beings who, plunged into meditation on *prakrti* or on *prakrti* animated by God, pierced the cosmic egg (mentally) and penetrated all the envelopes (*avarana*, "covers")—that is, all the levels of cosmic manifestation—to the primordial *Grund*, *prakrti* in its unmanifested mode, and who thus obtained the situation of Divinity.

Vyasa (on Y.S., III, 55) summed up the transition from *samprajnata* to *asamprajnata samadhi* thus: Through illumination (*prajna*, "wisdom") spontaneously acquired when the yogi is in the final stage of *samprajnata samadhi*, one achieves "absolute isolation" (*kaivalya*)—in other words, the liberation of the *purusha* from the clutch of *prakrti*. Vacaspati Misra in turn (on Y.S., I, 21) declared that the "fruit" of *samprajnata samadhi* was *asamprajnata samadhi*, and the "fruit" of the latter was *kaivalya*, deliverance. It would be wrong to regard this way of being of the spirit as a mere "trance" in which consciousness was devoid of all content. Undifferentiated enstasis is not the "absolute void." The "state" and the "knowledge" denoted at the same time by this term refer to the total absence of objects from consciousness and not at all to a consciousness emptied in an absolute fashion. For, on the contrary, the consciousness is saturated at that moment by a direct and total intuition of being. As Madhava said, "*nirodha* [the conclusive arrest of all psychomental experience] should not be imagined as a nonexistence, but rather as the support of a special condition of the spirit." It is the enstasis of total vacuity, without sensory content or intellectual structure, an unconditioned state that is no longer "experience" (for in it there no longer exists any rela-

To live no longer in time but in an eternal present

tion between consciousness and the world) but "revelation."
The intellect (*buddhi*), having accomplished its mission, withdraws, detaching itself from the *purusha*, and is reincorporated
into *prakrti*. The "human" consciousness is eliminated; in other
words, it no longer functions, its constituent elements having
been reabsorbed into the primordial substance. The yogi attains
to deliverance: a "death in life." He is *jivanmukta*, "the man
delivered in life." He no longer lives in time and under the
control of time, but in an eternal present, in the *nunc stans*
that was Boëtius' definition of eternity.

This would be the situation of the yogi in *asamprajnata
samadhi* as long as it was considered from without and judged
from the point of view of the dialectic of deliverance and the
relations between the Self and substance, as that dialectic was
developed by Samkhya. In reality, if the "experiences" of the
various *samadhis* are taken into consideration, the yogi's situation is more paradoxical and infinitely more splendid. Let us indeed take a closer look at what is meant by "reflection" of the
purusha. In this act of supreme concentration, "knowledge" is
tantamount to "appropriation." For revelation without the intercession of the *purusha* is at the same time the experimental
discovery of an ontological modality inaccessible to the layman.
This moment cannot be conceived of otherwise than as a paradox; for, once it has been achieved, it would be impossible any
longer in any way whatever to specify in what degree one can
still speak of the contemplation of the Self or of an ontological
transformation of man. The mere "reflection" of the *purusha* is
more than an act of mystic knowledge, inasmuch as it makes it
possible for the *purusha* to enjoy "mastery of itself." The yogi
takes possession of himself by means of an "undifferentiated
stasis" whose sole content is *being*. We should be guilty of be-
traying the Indian paradox if we reduced this "taking of possession" to a mere "knowledge of oneself," however profound
and absolute such knowledge might be. In actuality the "taking
of possession of oneself" radically alters the ontological system
of man. The "discovery of oneself," the self-reflection of the

purusha, entails a "rupture of level" on the cosmic scale: in consequence of its emergence, the modalities of the real are abolished, being (*purusha*) coincides with non-being ("man" properly so-called), knowledge is transformed into magic "mastery," thanks to the total absorption of the known by the knower. And, since this time the object of knowledge is pure Being, stripped of all form and attribute, it is the assimilation of pure Being to which *samadhi* leads. The self-revelation of the *purusha* is equivalent to a taking of possession of Being in all its amplitude. In *asamprajnata samadhi* the yogi is in effect the whole of Being.

Obviously his position is paradoxical: He is alive and yet delivered; he has a body and yet he knows himself and for this reason he *is* the *purusha;* he lives in time and simultaneously he shares in eternity; and he coincides with the whole of Being although he is only a fragment of it, etc. But the realization of this paradoxical situation has been the goal of Indian spirituality from its beginnings. What else are those "men-gods" of whom we spoke earlier except the "geometrical place" in which the divine and the human come together, as well as Being and Non-Being, Eternity and Death, the Whole and the Part? And India perhaps more than other civilizations has always lived beneath the sign of the "men-gods."

REINTEGRATION AND FREEDOM

Let us retrace the steps of this long and arduous journey proposed by Patanjali. Its goal is quite clear from the start: to emancipate man from his human condition, to win absolute freedom, to achieve the unconditioned. The method includes many techniques (physiological, mental, mystic), but all of them share a common trait: their anti-profane—rather, let us say, their anti-human character. The profane man lives in the world, marries, builds a family; yoga prescribes solitude and absolute chastity. The layman is "possessed" by his own life; the yogi refuses to "let himself live"; against the continuity of movement he sets his static position, the immobility of *asana*; to agitated, unrhythmic, multiformed respiration he opposes *pranayama*, and he dreams of achieving the total retention of breath; to the chaotic flux of psychomental life he replies with the "fixation of thought on a single point," the first step toward the definitive withdrawal from the world of phenomena that will be obtained by *pratyahara*. All the techniques of yoga summon us to the same act: to do exactly the opposite of what human nature forces us to do. From solitude and chastity to *samyama*, there is no solution of continuity. The orientation is always the same: to react against "normal," "profane," or, finally, "human" inclinations.

This total opposition to life is not new, either in India or elsewhere; it is easy to recognize in it the age-old, universal polarity of the sacred and the profane. The sacred has always been something "wholly other" than the profane. And, judged by this criterion, Patanjali's Yoga, like all the other yogas, contains a religious value. The man who repudiates his own condition and knowingly reacts against it, endeavoring to abolish it, is a man thirsting for the unconditioned, for freedom, for "power"; in a word, for one of the innumerable modalities of the sacred. This "reversal of all human values" that is pursued by the yogi is validated, moreover, by a long Indian tradition; for, from the Vedic point of view, the world of the gods is the diametrical opposite of ours (the god's right hand corresponds to man's left, an object broken here remains intact in the beyond, etc.). In his rejection of profane life the yogi is emulating a transcendent model: Isvara. And, even if the part played by God in the struggle for release is shown to be rather mediocre, this emulation of a transcendent modality retains its religious worth.

Let us point out that it is by stages that the yogi breaks his bonds with life. He begins by eliminating the least essential habits of living: comforts, amusements, the futile waste of time, the diffusion of his mental energies, etc. Then he endeavors to *unify* the most important functions of life: breathing, con-

sciousness. Disciplining his breathing, giving it a rhythm, reducing it to a single type—that of deep sleep—are tantamount
to the unification of all the varieties of respiration. On the level
of psychological life the same purpose is pursued by *ekagrata*:
fixating the flow of consciousness, achieving a psychic continuum
virgin of any fissure, "unifying" thought. Even the most elementary of the yogic techniques, *asana*, proposes a similar end:
If ever one is to succeed in becoming conscious of the "totality"
of one's body, felt as a "unity," one can do so only by experiencing one of these hieratic postures. The extreme simplification of life, calm, serenity, a static position of the body, the
maintenance of a rhythm in respiration, concentration on a
single point, etc.—all these exercises are directed toward the
same end, which is to eliminate multiplicity and fragmentation,
to reintegrate, to unify, to totalize.

All of this tells us to what a degree the yogi, withdrawing
from profane human life, finds another that is deeper and truer
—because it is "rhythmed": the very life of the cosmos. In fact
one might speak of the first stages of yoga as an effort toward
the "cosmicization" of man. In all the psychophysiological techniques from *asana* to *ekagrata* one senses the same ambition: the
transformation of the chaos of profane psychosomatic life into a
cosmos. One cannot achieve final liberation without knowing a
prior stage of "cosmicization"; one cannot go directly from
chaos to freedom. The intermediate phase is the cosmos—in
other words, the achievement of rhythm on all levels of psychosomatic life. Now this rhythm is shown to us in the structure of
the universe itself by the "unifying" function fulfilled in it by
the stars and especially by the moon.

Granted that this "cosmicization" is only an intermediate
phase, which is barely hinted at by Patanjali, but which is of
exceptional importance in the other Indian mystic schools. Attained after "unification," "cosmicization" continues the same
process: reshaping man in other, gigantic proportions, assuring
him of macranthropic experiences. But this macranthropos too
can have only a provisional existence. For the ultimate end will

Man and the cosmos: the pyramid-terraced *sakras* support at the summit the *bindu*, the seed of the universe

be attained only when the yogi succeeds in "withdrawing" into his own center and completely breaking all bonds with the cosmos, becoming impermeable to experience, unconditioned and autonomous. This final "withdrawal" is tantamount to a rupture of level, an act of real transcendence. *Samadhi* by its very nature is a paradoxical "state," for it empties being and thought and at the same time fills both to satiety. It goes without saying that the paradox is implied in the very function of the Indian ritual (as, for that matter, it is in every other ritual); for through the power of ritual any object can incorporate divinity, a "fragment" (in the instance of the Vedic sacrifice, a brick from the altar) coincides with the "Whole" (the god Prajapati), Non-Being with Being. Looked at from this point of view (that of the phenomenology of the paradox), *samadhi* is part of a well-known tendency in the history of religion and mysticism: that of the coincidence of opposites. It is true that this time the coincidence is not merely symbolic but concrete and experimental. Through *samadhi* the yogi transcends opposites and in a single experience he unites the empty and the overfull, life and death, being and non-being. And more: *samadhi*, like all paradoxical states, is equivalent to a reintegration of all the different modalities of the real in a single modality: the undifferentiated plenitude of the pre-Creation, primordial unity. The yogi who attains to *asamprajnata samadhi* also realizes a dream that has obsessed the human spirit since the dawn of its history: union with the Whole, the reconquest of Unity, the re-creation of the original nonduality, the abolition of time and the Creation (that is, cosmic multiplicity and heterogeneity); above all, the elimination of the bisection of the real into object and subject.

It would be a vulgar mistake to regard this supreme reintegration as a mere regression into the primordial chaos. It can never be repeated often enough that yoga, like so many other mysticisms, leads to the plane of paradox and not to a banal and easy extinction of consciousness. Since time immemorial India had known the innumerable "trances" and "ecstasies" obtainable through intoxication, narcotics, and all the other primitive means of emptying the consciousness. One has no right to include *samadhi* among these countless varieties of spiritual escape. Deliverance cannot be equated with the "deep sleep" of prenatal existence, even if it would appear that the reconquest of Totality obtained through undifferentiated enstasis resembles the bliss of the human being's fetal reconsciousness. One fact, which is of major importance, must always be taken into account: The yogi works on all levels of consciousness and the subconscious in order to open a path for himself to the transconscious (knowledge-possession of the Self, the *purusha*).

He penetrates into "deep sleep" and the "fourth state" (*turiya*, the cataleptic state) with the utmost lucidity, he is never bemused by self-hypnosis. The importance ascribed by all authors to the yogic states of *hyper*consciousness shows us that final reintegration is achieved in *this* direction and not in a "trance" of greater or lesser depth. In other words, the reconquest of the original nonduality through *samadhi* contributes this new element in relation to the primordial situation (the situation that existed before the real was bisected into object and subject): the *knowledge* of unity and blessedness. There is a "return to the source," but with this difference: The man "delivered in life" regains his original situation enriched by the dimensions of *freedom* and *transconsciousness*. In still other words, he does not automatically reconquer a "given" situation; he rejoins the original plenitude after having established this unprecedented and paradoxical mode of being: *the consciousness of freedom*, which exists nowhere in the cosmos, neither on the levels of life nor on the levels of "mythological divinity" (the gods, *deva*); which exists only in the Supreme Being.

It is here that one most esteems the initiatory character of yoga; for in initiation too one "dies" in order to "be reborn," but this new birth does not repeat the "natural birth"; the neophyte does not come back to the profane world to which he has just died during his initiation; he comes to a sacred world that corresponds to a new mode of being, *inaccessible to the "natural" (profane) level of existence*.

There is a temptation to see in this ideal—the conscious conquest of freedom—the justification offered by Indian thought for the fact—absurd and cruelly unnecessary on first glance—that the world exists, man exists, and his existence in the world is an uninterrupted sequence of illusions, sufferings, and despairs. For by delivering himself man establishes the spiritual dimension of freedom and "introduces" it into the cosmos and into life—in other words, into blind, wretchedly conditioned modes of existence.

Primordial plenitude and unity: Siva as Ardhanarisvara, at once man and woman (eighth-century Elephanta sculpture)

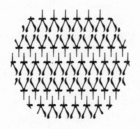

Ascetics, Ecstatics, and Contemplatives in Ancient India

ASCETICISM AND YOGA

As we have observed earlier, the *Yoga darsana* expounded by Patanjali and his commentators did not exhaust the whole of yogic ideology and techniques. Yoga is present everywhere in Indian spirituality, as much in the oral tradition as in the Sanskrit and vernacular literature. This is another way of saying that yoga constitutes a specific dimension of Indian spirituality, to such a degree that, when Christianity adjusted itself to Indian realities, it took over certain yogic methods of meditation and prayer. Moreover, many Indian scientists—sometimes almost without being aware of the fact—employ the yogic techniques of concentration.

The ascetic of the *Descent of the Ganges*. Cliff sculptures at Mahavalipuram (seventh century)

Yoga has succeeded in imposing itself as a pan-Indian technique by allying itself with two traditions: (1) that of the
ascetics and "ecstatics" attested to since the Rig Veda, and (2)
the symbolism of the Brahmana, particularly the speculations
that justified the "internalization of sacrifice." This millennial
process of integration, which culminated in one of the greatest
of India's spiritual syntheses, dramatically illustrates what has
been called the phenomenon of Hinduization.

In the Vedas one can find only rudiments of classical yoga.
On the other hand, these old texts lay much stress on ascetic
disciplines and "ecstatic" ideologies that, though they do not
always stand in direct relations with yoga properly so-called,
were finally incorporated into the yogic tradition.

The word *tapas* (literally, "warmth, ardor") denotes ascetic
endeavor in general (the term appeared as early as the Rig
Veda). *Tapas* was not reserved exclusively to the ascetics and
the "ecstatics." The sacrifice of the *soma* required of the
sacrificer and his wife certain rites of consecration including the
ascetic vigil, meditation in silence, fasting, and also "excitation,"
tapas—and these rites could last a day or a year. Now the *tapas*
that was achieved through fasting, vigils beside a fire, etc.,
could also be achieved by holding the breath. Especially with
the epoch of the Brahmana, holding the breath began to serve a
ritual function: When one chants the *Gayatrastrota*, it is
written in the Jaiminiya Brahmana (III, 3, i), one should not
breathe. According to other sources, a magic heat is produced
by holding the breath.

In order to sanctify oneself for the sacrifice of the *soma*, one
must practice *tapas* and become "on fire," the "magic heat"
being the supreme sign of transcendence of the human condition, emergence from the "profane." But heat can also be
produced by disciplining or holding the breath, and this makes
it possible on the one hand to assimilate the yogic techniques
to the orthodox Brahman methods and on the other to assimilate the yogi to the *tapasvin*, the man who practices asceticism.

Sacrifice was very early assimilated to *tapas*. The gods were supposed to have obtained immortality not only through sacrifice but also through asceticism. For *tapas* too is a "sacrifice." While in the Vedic sacrifice one offers the gods the *soma*, melted butter, and the sacred fire, in ascetic practice one offers them an "inner sacrifice" in which the physiological functions are substituted for libations and ritual objects. Respiration is often identified with an "uninterrupted libation." The *Vaikhanasasmarta Sutra* (II, 18) speaks of *pranagnihotra*—in other words, "daily sacrifice in respiration." *Pranayama* is identified with *agnihotra*, the oblation of fire that every master of a household was supposed to practice daily. The Brahman texts call the holding of the breath "inner *agnihotra*." For,

As long as he is speaking, a man cannot breathe, and then he is offering his breath to speech; as long as he is breathing, he cannot speak, and then he is offering his speech to breath. These are the two constant, immortal oblations; waking and sleeping, man offers them uninterruptedly. All the other oblations have a purpose and participate in the nature of the act [karma]. Knowing this true sacrifice, the ancients did not offer *agnihotra* [Kausitaki Brahmana *Up.*, II, 5].

In spite of its rough phraseology, this passage is not lacking in grandeur; a whole mystic physiology is embodied in it, for the physiological organs and functions are assimilated to operations that are at once ritual and spiritual. If one recollects that Indian ritual always implies a cosmic dimension, one sees that one is dealing with a multiple system of identifications and assimilations accomplished on various levels: cosmic, physiological, ritual, spiritual. This system of homologation was already to be found in the Vedas, but it was to triumph in conclusive fashion in Tantrism. Now one fact is worth underlining: It was above all through yogic techniques that Tantrism was organized as a coherent "system" with its own ideology and ritual. Then one recognizes the part played by yoga in the history of Indian spirituality: yoga "internalizes" ritual, it breathes a new value

into every fossilized form, it constantly readapts itself to the
ever new needs of the human spirit.

THE UPANISHADS AND YOGA

The Upanishads too, in their own way, reacted against ritualism.
The *rishis* of the Upanishads, exactly like the yogis, abandoned
ordinary life and Vedic "orthodoxy" in order to go in quest of
the absolute. It is true that the Upanishads remain within the
framework of metaphysics and contemplation, whereas yoga
employs asceticism and the meditative technique. But even so
the osmosis between the circles of yoga and those of the
Upanishads was never broken. Certain yogic methods, in fact,
were accepted by the Upanishads in the form of preliminary
exercises of purification and contemplation.

The word *yoga*, in its technical interpretation, is to be found
for the first time in the Taittiriya Upanishad, II, 4 (*yoga atma*)
and in the Katha Upanishad, II, 12 (*adhyatma yoga*), VI, 11
(the text closest to the classical meaning), but one can discern
the presence of yogic practice in the most ancient Upanishads.
Thus a passage of the Chandogya Upanishads, VIII, 15 ("concentrating all one's senses in oneself"), makes it possible to infer
the practice of *pratyahara*; similarly, *pranayama* is often found
in the Brhadaranyaka Upanishads (for instance, I, 5, 23).

Knowledge, in the Upanishads, brings deliverance from death:
"Lead me out of death to immortality!" (Brh. Up., I, 3, 28);
"Those who have knowledge of it become immortal" (Katha
Up., VI, 9; cf. VI, 18, *vimrtyu*, "liberated from death"). Yogic
practice as it was employed by the Upanishads pursued the
same end. And it is significant that, in the Katha Upanishads, it
is indeed Yama, the king of the dead, who reveals both supreme
knowledge and yoga at the same time. Even the story line of
this Upanishad (inspired, moreover, by an episode from the
Taittiriya Brahmana) is original and mysterious. Naciketas, a
young Brahman, arrives in hell and, having prevailed on Yama
to grant his three wishes, he asks to be instructed in the fate of

Naciketas inquires of Yama, the king of the dead, the secret of "the fire that leads to the sky" (modern popular drawing)

man after death. The descent into hell and the three days spent
there are well known initiatory themes: one is naturally re-
minded of the shaman initiations and of the mysteries of an-
tiguity. Yama gives Naciketas the secret of the "fire that leads
to heaven" (I, 14 ff.); a fire that can be regarded either as a
ritual fire or as a "mystic fire" produced by *tapas*. This fire is
"the bridge to the supreme *brahman*" (III, 2). The image of
the bridge, already so frequent in the Brahmana, recurs in the
most ancient Upanishads (cf. *Chand. Up.*, VIII, 4, 1–2); moreover, it is evidenced in many traditions and usually means the
initiatory passage from one to another mode of being (cf. my
Chamanisme, pp. 355 ff., 419 ff.). But above all it is the teaching
dealing with the "great journey" that is important. After vain
attempts to divert Naciketas from this problem by offering him
countless earthly rewards, Yama reveals to him the great mystery, the *atman*, which "cannot be attained by exegesis, or by
intellect, or by much study. Only he whom it chooses can
attain it" (II, 23, Renou's translation). The last line shows a
mystic trace, again marked in the next chapter by the reference
to Vishnu (III, 9).

The man in complete possession of himself is compared with
a skilled charioteer who knows how to dominate his senses: It
is such a man who gains deliverance.

Know that the *atman* is the master of the chariot, that the body is
the chariot itself, that reason is the charioteer, and that thought is
the reins. The senses are the horses, it is said, and the objects of the
senses are their course. . . . He who has knowledge and whose
thought is always harnessed has control of the senses: They are
like good horses for the driver. . . . He who has knowledge armed
with thought, who is always pure, will reach that place where one
is no longer born again [III, 3–4, 6, 8; Renou's translation].

Although yoga is not mentioned, the image is specifically
yogic: The team, the reins, the driver, and the good horses are
all related to the root-word *yuj*, "to grip tightly, to bring under

the yoke" (the same image occurs in the Maitrayani Up., II, 6).
And besides another verse makes it clear: "It is known under
the name of yoga, this firm control of the senses. Then one becomes concentrated . . ." (VI, ii; cf. VI, 18: "Then, having received this knowledge and total prescription of yoga, as imparted
by Death, Naciketas acceded to brahman and was exempt from
old age, exempt from dying").

IMMORTALITY AND DELIVERANCE

"The man who has knowledge for his driver and thought for
his reins reaches the other bank of the journey, the supreme
place of Vishnu," the Katha Upanishad says (III, 9). This is
not yet the Vishnu of the epic poems or that of the *Purana*, but
his part in this first Upanishad, in which yoga is employed in
order to gain the knowledge of the *atman* as well as immortality,
already points out the direction to be taken by the later great
syntheses. The three dominant avenues of deliverance—the
Upanishads' *knowledge*, yoga's technique, and *bhakti*—were
little by little to be homologated and integrated. This process
was even more advanced in an Upanishad of the same period,
the Svetasvatara, but instead of Vishnu it venerated Siva. Nowhere is the identity between mystic knowledge and immortality
more often expressed.

The predominance of the "theme of immortality" leads one
to believe that the Svetasvatara Upanishad was composed in a
"mystic" environment, or, rather, that it was rewritten in such
a circle, for its text has undergone numerous additions through
the centuries. The word *deliverance* is found less often in it
(IV, 16). But some passages speak of the joy that comes from
"the eternal happiness" gained by those who know Siva (VI,
12), an expression that, like so many others, reveals a concrete
content of true mystic experience. *Brahman* is identified with
Siva, whose name is also Hara (I, 10), Rudra (III, 2), and
Bhagavat (III, 11). We need not concern ourselves with the
composite structure, "sectarian" (Sivaist) in shading, of this

Upanishad. But it was necessary to emphasize its mystic experimental character (cf. also IV, 20) in order better to explain
the importance that it ascribes to yogic practices.

Thus yogic technique is incorporated into the tradition of the
Upanishads—a technique that offers considerable analogy with
that of the *Yoga Sutras*. Here are the essential passages:

Holding his body firm in the three erect parts (the trunk, the neck,
the head), sending his senses and his thought into his heart, a
wise man in the boat of *brahman* would cross all frightening rivers
[II, 8]. Having compressed the breath within the body, controlling
the movements, you must breathe through your nostrils at a reduced
rate; like a chariot drawn by bad horses, the wise man should
repress his thought without distraction [9]. Yoga should be practiced in a single pure place, without pebbles, fire, or sand, pleasing
to the inner sense in its sounds and its water, etc., which does not
offend the eye, protected from the wind by a hollow (in the
earth) [10]. Fog, smoke, sunshine, fire, wind, phosphorescent in-
sects, lightning, crystal, the moon are the preliminary aspects that
produce the manifestation of *brahman* in yoga [11]. When the
quintuple quality of yoga has been produced arising out of earth,
water, fire, wind, and space, there is no longer disease or old age or
death for him who has gained a body made of the fire of yoga [12].
Lightness, health, the lack of desires, clarity of skin, excellence of
voice, pleasant aroma, a reduction in the excretions—these are said
to be the first effects of yoga [13; all Silburn's translation].

In this passage one has recognized the three most important
angas of the *Yoga Sutras: asana, pratyahara,* and *pranayama.*
The acoustical and luminous phenomena that mark the stages
of yogic meditation and on which the later Upanishads were to
place much emphasis confirm the technical, experimental character of the secret tradition handed down by the Svetasvatara.
Another Upanishad of the same group, the Mandukya, contributes details concerning the four states of consciousness and
their relations with the mystic syllable OM. In addition, many

passages of the Maitri Upanishad emphasize meditation on this mystic syllable. OM is identical with Vishnu (VI, 23), with all the gods, with all air, with all sacrifices (VI, 5). By meditating on this mystic syllable one sees Brahma and obtains immortality (VI, 24); meditation leads to deliverance (VI, 22). "It is because in this way the yogi united *prana*, the syllable OM and this universe with all its innumerable forms . . . that this procedure is called *yoga*. The unity of respiration, consciousness, and the senses—followed by the annihilation of all concepts— is what yoga is" (VI, 25). He who labors correctly for six months will achieve perfect union (VI, 28). But this "secret" should be communicated only to one's sons and disciples, and only on condition that they are suitable to receive it (VI, 29).

THE YOGIC UPANISHADS

Among the nine (or, according to the collections, ten or eleven) yogic Upanishads, the most important are the Yogatattva, the Dhyanabindu, and the Nadabindu. It is the Yogatattva that seems to have the most minute knowledge of yogic practices: it mentions the eight *angas* and differentiates among the four kinds of yoga (Mantrayoga, Layayoga, Hathayoga, and Bajayoga). It pays considerable tribute to the magic prestige of the yogis. It mentions the four major *asanas* (*siddha*, *padma*, *simha*, and *bhadra*) and enumerates the obstacles encountered by beginners (these include laziness, garrulity, etc.). This is followed by a discussion of *pranayama* and rather important details of mystic physiology (the purifications of the passages is indicated by certain external signs: lightness of the body, the glow of the skin, increases in digestive power, etc.; the complete suspension of respiration is also evidenced by physiological symptoms, i.e., at the start of the practice, respiration becomes abundant, etc.). The power of rising into the air and that of controlling and dominating any other being whatever are immediate results of yogic practice. The yogi becomes handsome and strong as a god, and women desire him, but he should

Magic flight, an occult power of the male or female yogi. Detail from an eighteenth-century Tibetan painting representing the attributes of the *mahasiddas*

persevere in his chastity; "as a result of his retention of his sperm, the yogi's body is enveloped in a pleasing aroma." A long list of *siddhi*, occult powers, attests to the magic environment in which this Upanishad was developed; for it speaks of "second sight, second hearing, the possibility of transporting oneself over great distances in an instant, the ability to speak well, to assume any form, to become invisible, and the possibility of transmuting iron or other metals into gold by smearing them with excrement." This last *siddhi* clearly shows the real relations between a certain form of Yoga and alchemy.

The Yogatattva Upanishad displays a richer mystic philosophy than that of the *Yoga Sutras*. The "five parts" of the body correspond to the five cosmic elements (earth, water, fire, wind, and ether), and in addition there are a special mystic letter and a special *dharana*, governed by a god, to correspond to each of the elements; by achieving the meditation that applies to it, the yogi becomes the master of the element in question.

This Upanishad describes *samadhi* as the realization of the paradoxical situation in which the *jivatma* (the individual soul) and the *paramatma* (the universal spirit) are placed as soon as they become indistinguishable from each other. The yogi can then do whatever he likes; if he wishes, he can be absorbed into *parabrahma*; if, on the other hand, he wishes to retain his body, he can remain on earth and possess all the *siddhi*. He can also become a god, live in the midst of honors in heaven, and assume any shape that he wishes. The yogi who becomes a god can live as long as he likes.

In this Yogatattva Upanishad, then, one is dealing with a yogic technique that has been re-evaluated in the light of Vedantist dialectic; the *jivatma* and the *paramatma* take the places of the *purusha* and Isvara, the "Self" and "God." But what is even more significant than this Vedantist coloration is the experimental accent that is characteristic of this whole Upanishad. Its text retains the character of a technical manual with very precise instructions for the ascetic's use. The purpose pursued by this entire discipline is expressed comprehensively in it: to attain to the condition of the "man-god," unlimited longevity, and absolute freedom. This is the leitmotiv of all the popular versions of yoga, to which Tantrism was to give the greatest scope.

The Nadabindu Upanishad offers a rather detailed description of the auditory phenomena that accompany certain yogic exercises. In the beginning the sounds perceived are violent (similar to those of the ocean, thunder, or waterfalls); then they assume a musical structure, and finally hearing becomes very acute. The yogi should endeavor to hear sounds that are as rarefied as possible. At the final stage he will experimentally know union with *parabrahma*, which has no sound (*asabda*). This state of meditation is probably similar to a cataleptic state, inasmuch as the text asserts that "the yogi remains as if dead; he has been delivered (*mukta*)." In this *unmani* state (achieved at the instant when the yogi has transcended even mystic hearing) his body is "like a piece of wood: he feels neither heat nor cold, neither joy nor sorrow." He can no longer hear any sound.

The richest in technical instructions and "mystic" revelations among all the later Upanishads is undoubtedly the Dhyanabindu. Its magic, anti-devotional character leaps out from its earliest lines, in which it declares that a man's sins, however heinous, are annihilated by Dhyanayoga. This is exactly the point of view of extremist Tantrism: total emancipation with respect to all moral and social laws. The Dhyanabindu, exactly like the Nadabindu, begins with an iconographic description of the syllable OM. *Pranayama* too is identified with the three principal gods of the Vedic pantheon: "Brahma is said to be inhalation, Vishnu is retention (of the breath), Rudra is exhalation." At the same time the reader is advised to achieve *pranayama* by concentrating on the syllable OM.

"Subtle" physiology is particularly elaborated in this Upanishad. It specifies that the "lotus of the heart" has eight petals and thirty-two filaments. It ascribes a special value to *pranayama*; inhalation should be practiced through the three "mystic veins," *susumna, ida,* and *pingala,* and air should be

OM (A.U.M.) in Sanskrit

absorbed "between the eyelids," a place that is at once "the root of the nose and the habitation of immortality." This Upanishad mentions four *asanas*, seven *cakras* ("centers"), and ten names of *nadis* (the "veins" of Indian mystic physiology). It also tells of the "awakening" of Paramesvari, in other words Kundalini, a specifically Tantrist proceeding. There is also an element of erotic magic in it, a technique possessing certain analogies with the "orgiastic" movements of the *vamacaris* ("left-handed" Tantra) and the Sahajiya sect. These, obviously, are only indications, not precise, elaborated instructions. Thus, for example, the Upanishad guarantees that he who achieves *khecarimudra* "never loses his seed, even if he is embraced by a woman." (This then is a matter of withholding of seminal emission in the Tantrist fashion.) Later it states:

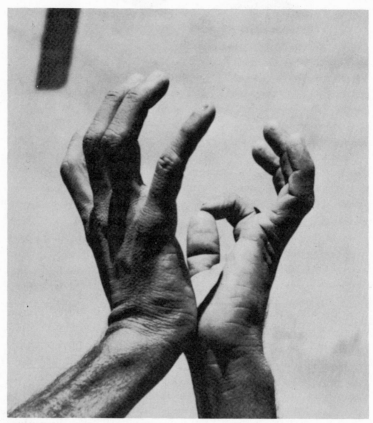

Padma mudra (the lotus symbol)

Yoni-lingam mudra (the symbol of ecstatic union)

The *bindu* [which in the secret language means *semen virile*] does not issue from the body as long as one practices *khecarimudra*. When the *bindu* reaches the genital area, it turns back, having been forced to do so by the power of *yonimudra*. This *bindu* is of two kinds: white and red. The white is called *sukla* [semen], while the name of the red is *maharajas*. The *rajas*, similar in color to coral, is found in the genital organs [Note: in the Yogic-Tantrist texts *rajas* means the secretion of the female genital organs.] The semen lives in the seat of the moon, midway between the *ajnacakra* [frontal region] and the lotus of a thousand petals [*sahasrara*]. Their union is most rare. The *bindu* is Siva and the *rajas* is Sakti; semen is the moon, *rajas* is the sun; through their union one gains a perfect body.

In the lexicon of Indian mystic eroticism all these terms have very precise meanings. This is primarily a case of the unification of the two polar principles (Siva and Sakti), of the transcendence of all opposites, achieved through a highly secret erotic practice. Let us point out then that this current of erotic magic, which was to be developed later in the Tantras, was not in the beginning foreign to yogic practices; that from the start these practices embodied many values and could be accepted and employed on multiple "paths."

The technical, experimental character of the Upanishads in the yogic group deserves to be emphasized. Here we no longer find the primacy of pure knowledge, of the dialectic of the Absolute as the sole instrument of deliverance. The identification of *atman* and *brahman* is no longer achieved through pure and simple concentration; on the contrary, it is realized experimentally, by means of an ascetic technique and a mystic physiology; in other words, by means of a process of transforming the human body into a cosmic body, in which the real veins, arteries, and organs play a definitely secondary part in relation to the "centers" and "veins" in which cosmic or divine forces can be experienced or "awakened." This tendency to the concrete and the experiential—even if "concrete" means the

The union of God and his *Sakti* (seventeenth-century Tibetan bronze)

almost anatomical localization of certain cosmic forces—is peculiar to the whole mystic current of the Indian Middle Ages. Devotion, personal worship, and mystic physiology here replace fossilized ritualism and metaphysical speculation. The road to deliverance tends to become an ascetic avenue, a technique that is learned with less difficulty than the Vedantist or Mahayanic metaphysics.

YOGA IN THE MAHABHARATA

Initially a heroic epic—and completed in this form probably during the seventh or sixth century before Christ—the Mahabharata has undergone innumerable interpolations. It is believed that particularly during the first two centuries of the Christian era a huge number of mystic-theological, philosophical, and juridical texts was introduced into the poem either in the form of complete wholes (Books XII and XIII, for instance) or as separate episodes. These diverse elements thus constitute a veritable encyclopedia of a marked Vishnuist tendency. One of the first portions to have been added to it (in all probability this occurred before the Christian Era) was the Bhagavad-Gita (in Book VI); the most important of these additions is found in Book VII, the Mokshadharma; and it is precisely in these books that one finds the most frequent allusions to yoga and Samkhya. It must not be forgotten, however, that these new portions, although introduced quite late, contain traditions far anterior to the date of their insertions.

Besought by Yudhisthira to explain the difference between the two paths, Bhisma replied (Mahabharata, XII, 11,043 ff.):

Samkhya and yoga alike flaunt each its own method as the best means . . . Those who choose to be guided by yoga base themselves on an immediate perception [of mystic essence]; those who follow Samkhya base themselves on traditional teachings. I consider both these doctrines true. . . . If their instructions are followed with precision, both will lead to the supreme end. They have in common purity, repression [of desires], and pity for all beings; the strict respect for oaths is common to both of them; but the opinions [*darsanas*] are not the same in Samkhya and in yoga.

The unsystematized character of these two ways to redemption is apparant. Even though one finds—particularly in the Gita and the Mokshadharma—such technical terms as *prakrti, tattva, mahat,* etc., nowhere is Samkhya presented as the method by which to differentiate the spirit from psychomental experience, the point of departure for the system of Isvara Krishna. Here Samkhya means only "true knowledge" (*tattva jnana*) or "knowledge of the Soul" (*atmabodha*); in this respect it affords analogies, rather, with the positions of the Upanishads. It is not that we are dealing with a "mixture of ideas from Samkhya and Vedanta," as Hopkins thought, but merely with a stage earlier than the Samkhya and Vedanta systems. Nor is it necessary to sift through certain portions of the Mahabharata for specific allusions to a theistic Samkhya school parallel to Isvara Krishna's atheistic *darsana*.

The Mokshadharma (verse 11,463) states that the precursors of the yogis are to be found in the Vedas (that is, in the Upanishads) and in Samkhya. In other words, the "verity" discovered by the Upanishads and Samkhya is accepted and assimilated by yoga, for this term—regardless of the meaning that is given to it—is applied above all to a spiritual technique. The Bhagavad-Gita goes even farther and assures us that "only limited minds, but not the wise, oppose Samkhya and yoga. He who is truly the master of either is sure of the fruit of both" (V, 4); "Samkhya and yoga are but one" (V, 5). This position is in complete accord with the spirit of the Bhagavad-Gita. For, as we shall not be slow in observing, in this key portion of the Mahabharata Krishna endeavored to integrate all the soteriological methods into one single new spiritual synthesis.

In the Mahabharata, yoga, in contrast to Samkhya, means every activity that leads the soul to Brahma while at the same time conferring innumerable "powers." Most often this activity

comes down to restraints on the senses, asceticism, and peni-
tences of every nature. Sometimes *yoga* means "method" (for
example, Gita, III, 3), occasionally "activity" (Mokshadharma,
verse 11,682), or "force" (verse 11,675 ff.), or "meditation"
(verse 11,691, etc.), or "renunciation" (*sannyasa*, as in the
Gita, VI, 2), etc. This diversity of meanings corresponds to a
real morphological diversity. If the word *yoga* means many
things, it is because yoga is many things. The Epic is in fact the
meeting-place of countless ascetic and popular traditions, each
equipped with a "yoga"—that is, a "mystic" technique—that is
peculiar to itself.

On a broad scale one can distinguish three classes of material
that can be of interest to us: (1) episodes of asceticism (*tapas*)
revealing practices and theories allied with Vedic asceticism and
without references to yoga properly so-called; (2) episodes and
discussions in which yoga and *tapas* are synonymous and both
are regarded as magic techniques; (3) episodes and didactic
passages in which yoga is presented with a terminology that is
its own and that is philosophically developed. It is particularly
the documents in this third category—largely embraced in the
Mokshadharma—that appear to be of interest to us because
they reveal certain forms of yoga for which insufficient material
can be found elsewhere.

One finds, for example, very ancient "magic" practices that
the yogis employed in order to influence and even to terrorize
the gods. The phenomenology of this magic asceticism is archaic: silence, excessive torture, the "desiccation of the body"
were among the means utilized not only by the yogis but also by
the kings (Mahabharata, I, 115, 24; 119, 7 and 34). In order to
make Indra give ground, Pandu remained standing on one foot
for a whole day and thus he finally won *samadhi* (I, 123, 26).
But this trance betrays no yogic content; it was rather a case of
a hypnosis produced by physical means, and the relations between man and god remained on the level of magic. Elsewhere
yoga is confused with pure asceticism, *tapas* (e.g., XII, 153, 36).
Yati (ascetic) and *yogi* become interchangeable terms and in

Ascetic standing on one foot: Baghirata seeking of Siva the
purifying descent of the Ganges (Mahavalipuram, seventh century)

the end are used indifferently to designate anyone "desirous of concentrating his spirit" whose object of study is not the Scriptures (*Sastra*) but the mystic syllable OM.

But, whatever the method selected, these practices are crowned by the acquisition of a force that our texts call "the force of yoga" (*yoga balam*). Its proximate cause is the "fixation of the spirit" (*dharana*), which is achieved through "placidity and equanimity" as well as through the progressive retardation of the rhythm of breathing (XII, 192, 13–14). In the passages inserted subsequently, the Mahabharata is rich in summaries and mnemonic patterns of yogic practices. Most of them reflect the traditional stereotypes:

A yogi who, in dedication to the great vow, skillfully fixates his rarefied spirit on the following places: navel, nape, head, heart, stomach, buttocks, eye, ear, and nose, hastily burning all good and evil deeds, be they like mountains [in size], and exerting every effort to attain to supreme yoga, is delivered [from the snares of existence] if such be his will [XII, 301, 39 ff.].

Another passage (V, 52 ff.) extols the difficulties of these practices and draws attention to the danger that threatens him who fails. "Hard is the great road and few are those who travel it to the very end, but great is called the guilt of him who, once engaged on the path of yoga, abandons its continuation and retraces his steps." This is the well-known danger of all magic actions, which unleash forces capable of killing the magician if he is not strong enough to subjugate them by his will and channel them according to his desire. An impersonal, sacred force is set loose by the yogi's asceticism, similar to the energies released by any other magic or religious ceremonial act.

The magic character of the yogic practices is also emphasized at other points. It is explained, for example, that he who enjoys the most perfect carnal felicities is not the Brahman but the yogi; even on earth, during his ascetic apprenticeship, the yogi is served by phosphorescent women, but in heaven he enjoys tenfold all the delights that he had renounced on earth (XIII, 107).

THE MESSAGE OF THE BHAGAVAD-GITA

The Bhagavad-Gita, one of the earliest major interpolations in Book VI of the Mahabharata, ascribes an importance of the highest order to yoga. Obviously the yoga expounded and recommended by Krishna in this masterwork of Indian spirituality is not the classical yoga of Patanjali or the collection of "magic" techniques that we have encountered thus far, but a yoga revised for the Vishnuist religious experience: a method intended for the acquisition of the *unio mystica*. If one considers the fact that the Bhagavad-Gita represents not only the peak of ecumenical Indian spirituality but also a vast attempt at synthesis, in which all the "paths" to salvation are validated and incorporated into Vishnuist devotion, the importance that Krishna gives to yoga here is tantamount to a veritable triumph of the yogic tradition. The strong theistic coloration given to it by Krishna greatly assists us in understanding the function fulfilled by yoga in the whole of Indian spirituality. Two conclusions, in fact, arise out of this observation: (1) Yoga can be understood as a discipline whose goal is the union of the human and the divine souls; (2) it is in this way—that is, as a "mystic experience"—that yoga has been understood and applied in the great popular "sectarian" devotional movements that have their echoes in the interpolations in the Mahabharata.

There is not space here to launch into a detailed analysis of the Bhagavad-Gita. In sum, Krishna reveals the "imperishable yoga" to Arjuna, and his revelations deal with: (1) the structure of the universe; (2) the modalities of being; (3) the roads to be followed in order to arrive at final deliverance. But Krishna is careful to add that this "antique yoga," which is the "supreme mystery," is not an innovation: He had earlier taught it to Vivasvat, who subsequently revealed it to Manu, and Manu transmitted it to Iksvaku (IV,.1). "It was through this tradition that it was conveyed to the *rishi*-kings; but, in the course of time, this yoga disappeared from the earth" (VI, 2). Whenever order (*dharma*) is troubled, Krishna manifests himself (IV, 7): that is, he reveals this timeless wisdom in a manner appropriate to the particular "historical moment." According to the Indian tradition so forcefully reaffirmed by Krishna, the various "historical moments"—which at the same time are moments of cosmic "becoming"—do not *create* the doctrine, they merely bring forth *appropriate formulas* of the timeless message. This is the same as saying that, in the case of the Bhagavad-Gita, its "innovations" are explained by the historical moment, which called specifically for a new and more immense spiritual synthesis. On the point that concerns us here—the meaning that the poem ascribes to the yogic techniques—let us point out only that the major problem of the Bhagavad-Gita is to determine whether *action* too can lead to the acquisition of salvation or whether *mystic meditation* is the only means of attaining it. In other words, it is the conflict between "action" (karma) and "contemplation" (*sama*). Krishna tries to overcome this dilemma (which, beginning in the era immediately subsequent to the Vedas, has uninterruptedly obsessed Indian spirituality) by showing that the two methods set off in opposition to each other were equally valid, since each individual could direct his choice to that method that his current karma made it possible for him to apply: either "action," then, or knowledge and mystic contemplation. It is here that Krishna calls on "yoga"; a yoga that was not yet Patanjali's *darsana* but that was also no longer the "magic" yoga to which other parts of the Mahabharata refer.

KRISHNA, THE EXEMPLARY MODEL

It might be said that the essence of the doctrine revealed by Krishna is epitomized in this curt formula: Understand Me and emulate Me! For everything that he revealed of his own being and his "behavior" in the cosmos and in history was supposed to serve Arjuna as an exemplary model. Arjuna discovered the meaning of his historical life and at the same time obtained deliverance by understang what Krishna *is* and what he *does*. Moreover, Krishna himself insisted on the exemplary and redemptive value of the divine model: "Everything that is done by the Leader is emulated by other men: The rule that he observes is followed by the world" (III, 21). And, referring to himself, he adds: "In the three worlds there is nothing that I am bound to do . . . and yet I remain in action" (III, 23). Krishna hastened to lay bare the deeper significance of this activity: "If I were not always tirelessly in action everywhere, men would follow my example. The worlds would cease to exist if I did not accomplish my work; I should be the cause of universal confusion and the end of all creatures" (III, 23–24; É. Sénart's translation).

Consequently Arjuna was supposed to emulate Krishna's behavior: first of all, to continue to act in order not to contribute through his passivity to "universal confusion." But, in order that he be able to act "in the manner of Krishna," he must understand the essence of divinity as well as its modes of manifestation. That is why Krishna *reveals himself*: By knowing God, man knows at the same time the model that he must follow. Now Krishna begins by revealing that Being and Non-Being reside in him and that the whole of the Creation—from the gods to the minerals—descends from him (VII, 4–6; IX, 4–5, etc.). He is constantly creating the world by means of his *prakrti* (IX, 8), but this incessant activity does not chain him (IX, 9): he is only the spectator of his own creation (IX, 10). Now it is precisely this apparently paradoxical evaluation of activity (karma) that constitutes the major lesson of yoga revealed by Krishna: By emulating God, who creates and sustains the world without taking part in it, man will learn to do likewise. "It is not enough to abstain from action in order to liberate oneself from the act: Inaction alone does not lead to perfection," for "everyone is condemned to action" (III, 4–5). It is useless for man to rein the activity of his senses, for "he whose soul is

Krishna, "the Black," the protector of the Pandavas, listens to the prayer of one of their number (the second from the left is Arjuna, with his bow). An episode from the Mahabharata (sixteenth-century Mogul painting)

troubled by the evocation of perceptible objects"—in other words, the generality of men—cannot succeed in detaching himself from the world. Even if he abstains from acts in the strict sense of the word, a whole unconscious activity produced by the *gunas* (III, 5) continues to bind him to the world and to incorporate him into the karmic circuit.

Condemned to action—for "action is superior to inaction" (III, 8)—man should perform the acts prescribed (in other words, the "duties," the acts that are incumbent on him by virtue of his particular situation). "It is better to perform one's own duty [*svadharma*], even imperfectly, than to perform, even perfectly, the duty of another condition [*paradharma*]" (III, 35). These specific activities are conditioned by the *gunas* (XVII, 8 ff.; XVIII, 23 ff.). On a number of occasions Krishna repeats that the *gunas* originate with him but do not bind him: "It is not I that am in them; it is they that are in me" (VII, 12). "I have created the division into four classes that distinguish the *gunas* . . . and yet I am inactive, immutable" (IV, 13). The lesson that emerges from this is the following: Even though accepting the "historical situation" created by the *gunas* (and one ought to accept it, for the *gunas* too derive from Krishna) and acting in accordance with the necessities of that "situation," man ought to refuse to *evaluate* his acts and, consequently, to ascribe an *absolute value* to his own condition. In other words, he should on the one hand deny ontological reality to any human "situation" (for only Krishna is saturated in Being) and on the other hand restrain himself from enjoying "the fruits of his actions."

"ACTS" AND "SACRIFICES"

In this sense it might be said that the Bhagavad-Gita endeavors to "save" all human acts, to "justify" every profane action; for, by the very fact that he no longer enjoys their "fruits," man transforms his acts into *sacrifices*—that is, into transpersonal dynamisms that contribute to the preservation of

the cosmic order. Now, as Krishna points out, only those acts
the object of which is sacrifice do not bind: "Act, then, only
when casting off every tie" (III, 9). Prajapati created sacrifice
in order that the cosmos might be able to manifest itself and
human beings might be able to live and reproduce themselves
(III, 10 ff.). But Krishna reveals that man too can collaborate in
the perpetuation of the divine work: not only by sacrifices properly so-called (those that constitute the Vedic ritual) but by
all his acts, whatever their nature. For him who "busies himself
in works of sacrifice, all activity is dissolved into nothingness"
(IV, 23). This means that activity no longer "enchains," no
longer creates new karmic nuclei. It is in this sense that the
various ascetics and yogis "sacrifice" their physiological and
psychic activities: They *detach* themselves from these activities,
they give them a *transpersonal* value; and, by so doing, "all
enjoy the real concept of sacrifice, and, through sacrifice, they
erase their stains" (IV, 25–30).

This transmutation of profane into ritual activities is made
possible by yoga. Krishna reveals to Arjuna that the "man of
action" can be saved, can escape the consequences of his participation in the life of the world, *even while continuing to act.*
The "man of action" means the man who cannot withdraw
from secular life in order to gain his salvation by means of
knowledge or mystic devotion. The only thing that he should
observe is this: *He should detach himself from his acts and
their consequences*; in other words "renounce the fruits of his
acts" (*phalatrishnavairagya*), *act impersonally*, without passion,
without desire, as if he were acting as a proxy, on behalf of
another. If he conforms rigorously to this rule, his acts will
implant no further seeds of karmic potentialities, nor will they
longer subjugate him to the circuit of karma. "Indifferent to
the action's fruit, always satisfied, free of all attachments, however occupied he may be, in reality he is not acting . . ."
(IV, 20).

The great originality of the Bhagavad-Gita is its emphasis on
this "yoga of action," which is achieved by "renouncing the

fruits of one's acts" (*phalatrishnavairagya*). This is also the major reason for its unprecedented success in India. For it was now licit for every man to hope that he would be saved through *phalatrishnavairagya* even if, for reasons of very varied kinds, he were still obliged to continue his participation in social life, to rear a family, to have worries, to hold office, even to commit "immoral" acts (like Arjuna, who had to kill his enemies in war). To act calmly, automatically, without being moved by "desire for the fruit" is to gain a mastery of self and a serenity that undoubtedly yoga alone can confer. As Krishna says, "Even while acting without restrictions he remains faithful to yoga." This interpretation of yogic technique, in which we are shown an instrument that makes it possible to detach oneself from the world even while continuing to live in it and act in it, is characteristic of the vast endeavor of synthesis undertaken by the author of the Bhagavad-Gita, which sought to reconcile all the vocations (ascetic, mystic, active) as earlier it had reconciled Vedantic monism with the pluralism of Samkhya; but it attests at the same time to the flexibility of yoga, which thus demonstrates once more that it can adapt itself to all religious experiences and satisfy all needs.

YOGIC TECHNIQUE IN THE BHAGAVAD-GITA

In addition to this "yoga" available to everyone, which consists in the renunciation of the "fruits of acts," the Bhagavad-Gita briefly explains a yogic technique, properly so-called, that is reserved to the *munis* (VI, 11 ff.). Although morphologically (in bodily positions, fixation on the end of the nose, etc.) this technique is similar to that exponded by Patanjali, the meditation of which Krishna speaks is different from that of the *Yoga Sutras*. First of all, *pranayama* is not mentioned in this context. (Gita, IV, 29, and V, 27, refers to *pranayama*; but here, rather than a yogic exercise, it is a meditation of substitution, an "internalized ritual," like those found at the period of the Brahmana and the Upanishads.) In the second place, yogic medita-

tion in the Gita achieves its supreme goal only if the yogi concentrates himself in Krishna.

"His soul serene and without fear, constant in his vow to
keep to the path of chastity [*brahmacari*], his intellect firm and
thinking unceasingly of Me, he should practice yoga taking Me
as his supreme end. Thus, his soul constantly devoted to meditation and his intellect subjugated, the yogi gains the peace that
dwells in Me and whose ultimate limit is nirvana" (VI, 14–15).
The mystic devotion (*bhakti*) whose object is Krishna gives
him an infinitely greater *role* than Isvara's in the *Yoga Sutras*.
In the Gita Krishna is the sole goal; it is he who justifies yogic
practice and meditation, it is in him that the yogi "concentrates
himself"; it is through his grace (and in the Gita the concept
of grace is already beginning to take shape, foreshadowing the
luxuriant development that it was to have in Vishnuist literature) that the yogi gains the nirvana that is neither the nirvana
of later Buddhism nor the *samadhi* of the *Yoga Sutras*, but a
state of perfect mystic union between the soul and its God.

A true yogi easily attains to the infinite blessedness produced
by contact with Brahma (VI, 28). The invocation of Brahma
in a text that is an apologia for Krishna should not surprise us.
In the Bhagavad-Gita Krishna is the pure Spirit: the "great
Brahma" is only his "matrix" (*yoni*) (XIV, 3). "I, I am the
Father, he who gives seed" (XIV, 4). Krishna is "the support
of Brahma," just as he is that of immortality, of imperishability,
of eternal order and perfect happiness (XIV, 27). But, although
in this context Brahma is transplanted to the "feminine" condition of *prakrti*, his nature is of a spiritual character. The *muni*
attains to him through yoga (V, 6). The "infinite blessedness"
that results from the union with Brahma enables the Yogi to
see "the soul (*atman*) in all beings and all beings in the *atman*"
(VI, 29). And, in the next strophe, it is specifically in Krishna's
identification with the *atman* of beings that the mystic bond
between the yogi and the god finds its basis: "Him who sees
Me everywhere and sees all things in Me I will never abandon,
and never will he abandon Me. He who, having fixated himself

Bhakti

in unity, adores Me who inhabit all beings, this yogi inhabits Me, whatever his way of life" (VI, 30–31). In the Isa Upanishad (Chap. VI) one encounters the same theme as in the strophe quoted above (Gita, VI, 30), and this shows that in the Upanishads there were theistic currents that have been bequeathed to the Gita, in which they have been so magnificently developed. Krishna, a personal god and the source of the true mystic experiences (*bhakti*), is here identified with the Brahma of the purely speculative metaphysics of the most ancient Upanishads.

The most lavish praises of the Gita, however, are heaped not on the yogi wholly detached from the suffering and the illusions of this world but on him who regards the pain and the joy of others as his own (VI, 32). This is a leitmotiv of Indian and above all of Buddhist mysticism. The sympathy of the author of the Bhagavad-Gita goes out in its entirety to him who practices such a yoga. If he fails in this life, he will be reborn into a family of skillful yogis and in another life he will succeed in perfecting what he could not bring to a fruitful conclusion in this life (VI, 41). Krishna reveals to Arjuna that only the fact of having attempted the path of yoga raises one man above another who has clung to the practice of the rites prescribed by the Vedas (VI, 44). And Krishna does not omit to mention that, among the roads that lead to salvation, the best and the most to be recommended is the way of yoga: "Yoga is superior to asceticism [*tapas*], superior even to knowledge [*jnana*], superior to sacrifice" (VI, 46).

This is the total triumph of yogic practices. Not only are they accepted by the Bhagavad-Gita, that summit of Indian spirituality; they are also elevated to the first rank. It is true that this yoga is purged of its vestiges of magic (rigorous asceticism, etc.) and that the most important of its ancient techniques, *pranayama*, now plays only an insignificant part. It is true too that here meditation and concentration become instruments of *unio mystica* with a god who reveals himself as a person. But in spite of this the acceptance of yogic practices by the Vishnuist mystic and devotional current proves the considerable popularity of these practices and also their Indian universality. Krishna's discourse is tantamount to his endorsement, in the presence of the whole of Hinduism, of a devotional yoga, of yogic technique regarded as a purely Indian means of obtaining mystic union with the personal god. A vast part of the modern yogic literature published in India and elsewhere finds its theoretical justification in the Bhagavad-Gita.

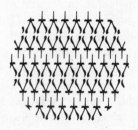

Buddhism, Tantrism, Hathayoga

YOGA AND NIRVANA

During his period of study and asceticism, Sakyamuni had learned the Samkhya doctrines as well as the yogic practices. In Vaisali, Arada Kalama taught a kind of preclassic Samkhya and Udraka Ramaputra explained the fundamentals and the aims of yoga. If Buddha refused the teachings of these two masters, it was because he had gone beyond them. But, as Émile Sénart wrote as early as 1900, Buddha did not repudiate the Indian ascetic and contemplative traditions as a whole; he enhanced them: "It was on the soil of yoga that Buddha was brought up; whatever new elements he might have been able to infuse into it, it was the world of yoga in which his thinking was shaped" (Sénart, *Bouddhisme et Yoga*, p. 348).

Before he became Buddha, Sakyamuni tried to find his way through asceticism

At first sight, Buddha rejected Brahman orthodoxy and the speculative tradition of the Upanishads as well as the innumerable mystic-ascetic "heresies" evolved on the fringe of Indian society. And yet the central problem of Buddhism, suffering and the release from suffering, is the traditional problem of Indian philosophy. This apparently paradoxical situation becomes more understandable if one reflects that Buddha proposed to go beyond all the philosophical formulas and mystic prescriptions in vogue in his time in order to deliver man from their control and open the "way" for him to the Absolute. If he appropriated the merciless analysis to which preclassic Samkhya and yoga subjected the idea of "person" and psychomental life, it was because the "Self" had nothing to do with that illusory entity, the human "soul." But Buddha went even farther than Samkhya, yoga, and the Upanishads, for he refused to postulate the existence of a *purusha* or an *atman*. In fact, he denied the possibility of having even an approximate experience of the true Self as long as a man remained "unawakened." Buddha also rejected the conclusions of the speculation of the Upaḥshads: the postulate of a *Brahma*, pure Spirit, Absolute, Immortal, Eternal, identical with the *atman*; but he did so because this dogma threatened to satisfy the intelligence and consequently prevented man from awakening.

On closer examination of the matter, one becomes aware that Buddha rejected all contemporary philosophies and asceticisms because he regarded them as *idola mentis* that erected a screen between man and absolute reality, the one true unconditioned essence. A number of canonical texts prove that Buddha in no way envisaged the negation of an ultimate, unconditioned reality beyond the flux of cosmic and psychomental phenomena; these texts show that he refrained from dwelling at too great length on the subject. Nirvana is the height of the absolute, *asamskrta*—in other words, what is neither born nor made, what is irreducible, transcendent, beyond all human experience.

It would be futile to contend that nirvana does not exist because it is not an object of knowledge. Undoubtedly nirvana is not known directly in the way in which color, sensation, etc., are known; it is not known indirectly through its activity in the way in which the sensory organs are known. Its nature, however, and its activity . . . are objects of knowledge. . . . The yogi enters into contemplation . . . [and] takes cognizance of nirvana, of its nature, of its activity. When he emerges from contemplation, he cries: "O Nirvana! destruction, calm, excellence, release!" The blind, since they do not see blue and yellow, have no right to say that the sighted do not see colors and that colors do not exist [*Samghabhadra*, quoted by L. de La Vallée-Poussin in *Nirvâna*, Paris, 1925, pp. 73–74 cf. *Visuddhimagga*, p. 507: "One cannot say that a thing does not exist because fools do not perceive it."]

Nirvana can be "seen" only with "the eyes of the saints"—that is, with a transcendent "organ" that is no longer part of the perishable world. The problem for Buddhism, as for any other initiation, was to show the way and to create the means of obtaining this transcendent "organ" that could reveal the unconditioned.

Let us remember that Buddha's message was addressed to the man who suffers, the man caught in the nets of transmigration. For Buddha, as for all forms of yoga, salvation was to be gained only at the end of a personal effort, a concrete assimilation of truth. This was neither a *theory* nor an escape into a random *ascetic effort*. Truth must be *understood* and at the same time *experienced*. Now both ways entailed risks: "understanding" might remain a mere speculation and "experimentation" might lead to ecstasy.

To Buddha one could find salvation only by attaining to nirvana—that is, by transcending the level of profane human experience and rejoining the level of the unconditional. But Buddha hesitated to speak of this unconditioned in order not to do it injustice. If he attacked the Brahmans and the *paribbajakas*, it was precisely because they descanted too much on the inexpressible and professed to be able to define the Self (*atman*). To Buddha, "the argument that the *atman* exists really and permanently is a false view; the argument that it does not exist is a false view" (Vasubandhu). But, if we read what he said of the delivered man, the man who had attained nirvana, we shall see that in every respect this man resembles "the man delivered in life," the non-Buddhist *jivanmukta*. "Even in this life" he is "withdrawn, given nirvana, feeling happiness in himself, and he spends his time with his soul identified with Brahma" (*Anguttara Nikaya*, II, 206). L. de La Vallée-Poussin, who quoted this passage, cited the Bhagavad-Gita, V, 24: "He who find happiness, joy, light only within, the yogi identified with Brahma, attains to nirvana, which is Brahma (*brahmanirvanam*)." Thus we see the direction in which Buddha extended the Indian mystic-ascetic tradition: He believed in a "deliverance in life," but he refused to define it. "If Buddha refused to explain himself on the subject of the Man Delivered, it was not because even the living saint did not really exist but because one can say nothing precise about the Man Delivered" (de La Vallée-Poussin, *op. cit.*, p. 112). All that can be said of the *jivanmukta* (or, in Buddhist terminology, the "nirvana-ed") is that he is not of this world. "The *Tathagata* can no longer be described as being matter, sensations, ideas, desires, knowledge: he is delivered from these designations; he is profound, immeasurable, unplumbable as the great ocean. One cannot say: 'he is,' 'he is not,' 'he is and is not,' 'he neither is nor is not'" (*Samyutta Nikaya*, IV, 374). This is precisely the speech of negative mysticism and theology, it is the famous *Neti! Neti!* of the Upanishads.

BUDDHIST ASCETICISM

In order to attain to the unconditioned state—in other words, to die at the root to this profane, suffering, illusory life and be reborn into the mystic life that will make access to nirvana possible—Buddha employed the yogic techniques. The preliminaries of Buddhist asceticism and meditation are similar to those recommended by the *Yoga Sutras* and other classic texts. The ascetic should choose a secluded place—in a forest, at the foot of a tree, in a cave, in a cemetery, or even on a haystack in the middle of a field—arrange himself in the position of *asana*, and begin his meditation.

Rejecting thirst for the world, he is left with a heart free from desire and he purges his spirit of covetousness. Rejecting the desire to harm, he is left with a heart free from enmity, with good will and compassion toward all beings, and he purges his spirit of ill will. Rejecting laziness and sloth, he is left delivered from both; conscious of the light, lucid and master of himself, he purges his spirit of laziness and sloth. . . . Rejecting doubt, he is left like one who has gone beyond perplexity; no longer uncertain what is good, he purges his spirit of doubt [Dighanikaya, III, 49].

Although it includes "moral" elements, this meditation has no ethical meaning. Its aim is to purge the ascetic's consciousness, to prepare it for loftier spiritual experiences. Yogic meditation as it is construed by Buddha in certain passages of the Dighanikaya has as its specific purpose to "remake" the ascetic's consciousness; that is, to create for him a new "immediate experience" of his psychic and even of his biological life. Through all his concrete actions—his gait, the position of his body, his breathing, etc.—the ascetic must rediscover in concrete fashion the "verities" revealed by the Master; in other words, he must transform all his movements and all his actions into pretexts for meditation. The Dighanikaya (II, 291 ff.) stipulates that, having chosen a solitary place for his meditation, the *bhikku* should take cognizance of all his physiological acts that hitherto he carried out automatically and unconsciously. "By drawing long breaths he will thoroughly understand this long inhalation; by exhaling briefly, he will undersand, etc. And he exerts himself to be conscious of all his exhalations, . . . of all his inhalations; and he exerts himself to retard his exhalations . . . and his inhalations."

This procedure is in no way a mere exericise in *pranayama*, it is a meditation on the Buddhist "verities," a permanent ex-

perimentation in the non-reality of matter. For this is the aim
of meditation: the complete assimilation of the fundamental
"verities" and their transformation into a "continuing experience," their diffusion, so to speak, through the monk's entire
being. Here indeed is what the same passage of the Dighanikaya
asserts later (II, 292):

. . . Whether walking forward or backward, an ascetic has complete understanding of what he is doing; looking or looking fixedly
(at an object), he completely understands what he is doing; raising
or lowering his arm, he completely understands what he is doing;
wearing his cloak or his other garments or carrying his food bowl, he
completely understands what he is doing; eating, drinking, chewing,
tasting, . . . evacuating, . . . walking, sitting, sleeping, waking,
speaking, or being silent, he completely understands what he is
doing.

The purpose toward which this lucidity is directed is easy to
understand. Unremittingly, no matter what he is doing, the
bhikku should undersand both his body and his soul, in order
constantly to realize the brittleness of the phenomenal world
and the unreality of the "soul." The commentary entitled *Sum-
angala Vilasini* draws this conclusion from meditation on bodily
movements: "They say that it is a living entity that walks, a
living entity that rests; but is there really a living entity that
walks or rests? There is none."

But this unbroken attention to one's own physiological life,
this technique for the annihilation of the illusions created by
a false conception of the "soul," are only preliminaries. True
Buddhist meditation begins with the experience of the four
psychic states called *jhana* (cf. Sanskrit *dhyana*). It was in the
Dighanikaya (I, 182 ff.) that the technique of Buddhist meditation was formulated, if not for the first time (though this is
quite probable), at least most clearly. Let us reproduce some
fragments from this major docment:

When the *bhikku* perceives that the five fetters [sensuality, ill will, laziness, agitation, doubt] have been destroyed in him, he is glad; glad, he is joyous; joyous, he feels at ease in his whole person; having this feeling of well-being, he is happy; happy, his heart is appeased. Released from desires and from all evil conditions, he enters into and he remains in the first *jhana*, a state that is born of detachment [*vivekaja:* "born of solitude"], in which reflection and understanding continue, in which one knows joy and bliss. Then the idea of the desires that he formerly had ceases in him and there arises the subtle, real idea of the joy and the peace that are born of detachment; and he remains in this idea.

Then,

through the elimination of reflection and understanding, the *bhikku* enters into the second *jhana*, which, born of concentration, is characterized by inner tranquilization, unification of the spirit, joy and bliss. Then the subtle, real idea of the joy and bliss born of detachment vanishes in him and there arises the subtle, real idea of the joy and bliss born of concentration; and he remains in this idea.

Next the *bhikku*,

through the renunciation of joy, remains indifferent. Alert and fully conscious, he experiences in his person that bliss of which the sages speak when they say: "He who is indifferent and thoughtful enjoys bliss." This is the third *jhana*. At this moment the subtle, real idea of the joy and peace that he felt before and that were born of concentration vanishes in him, and there arises a subtle, real idea of bliss and indifference.

After this, renouncing all feeling of ease and unease, through the end of the joy and affliction that he experienced earlier, the *bhikku* enters into and remains in the fourth *jhana*, a state of absolute purity, indifference, and thought without ease and without unease. [Physiologically the fourth *jhana* is characterized by the stoppage of

At Bodh-Gaya (where Buddha received his illumination)·

At Borobudur (Java, seventh century)

respiration.] That subtle, real idea of bliss and indifference that he
had earlier vanishes then in him and there arises a subtle, real idea
of the absence of ease and of unease, and he remains in this idea
[Dighanikaya, I, 182 ff.; Oltramare's translation].

We shall not cite more passages dealing with these four
jhanas. The stages are sufficiently clearly set forth: (1) purging
intelligence and sensitivity of "temptations"—in other words,
isolating them from external forces; in a word, gaining an initial
autonomy of consciousness; (2) eliminating the dialectical functions of the intelligence, obtaining concentration, the perfect
mastery of a rarefied consciousness; (3) suspending all "relation"
both with the outer world and with memory, achieving a placid
lucidity with no content other than the "consciousness of existing"; (4) rejoining "opposites," winning the blessedness of
"pure consciousness."

But the journey does not end here. We must add four
spiritual exercises that are called *samapattis*, "gains," and that
prepare the ascetic for the final "enstasis." In spite of the detailed description of them that is provided, these "states" are
difficult to understand. They correspond to experiences too remote not only from those of normal consciousness but also from
the extrarational (mystic or poetic) experiences that are comprehensible to Western minds. Yet it would be inaccurate to
explain them by hypnotic inhibitions. During the meditation the
monk's rationality is constantly verified; furthermore, sleep and
the hypnotic trance are obstacles that were very well known to
the Indian writers on meditation and against which the ascetic
was constantly kept vigilant. Here is how the four *samapattis*
are described:

And now, going beyond the notions of form, putting an end to the
notions of contact, ridding his spirit of distinct ideas, thinking:
"Space is infinite," the *bhikku* reaches and remains in the region of
the infinity of space, Proceeding next beyond the region of the
infinity of space and thinking: "Consciousness is infinite," he

reaches and remains in the region of the infinity of consciousness. [Note: Consciousness is shown to be infinite once it is no longer confined by sensory and mental experiences.] Then, going beyond the region of the infinity of consciousness and thinking: "There is nothing," he reaches and remains in the region of the non-existence of anything. Finally, going beyond the region of non-existence, the *bhikku* reaches and remains in a state of spirit that is neither idea nor the absence of idea [Dighanikaya, I, 183 ff.; Oltramare's translation].

It would be fruitless to comment on each of these stages, utilizing the rich texts of later Buddhist literature, unless one wanted to reconstruct the psychology and the metaphysics of the school. But, since what concerns us here is essentially the morphology of meditation, let us proceed to the ninth and last *samapatti*.

In truth, once the *bhikku* has had these ideas from himself [being in *dhyana*, he cannot derive ideas from without], he goes from one degree to the next, and so on, until he has attained to the supreme idea. And, when he has arrived there, he says to himself: "To think is worse; not to think is better. If I think, I fashion. It is possible that these ideas may vanish and that other ideas, which would be coarse, may be born. That is why I will no longer think or fashion." And he no longer thinks or fashions. And, since he no longer thinks or fashions, the ideas that he had disappear without other, coarser ideas coming into being. He has achieved cessation [Dighanikaya, I, 184; Oltramare's translation].

Another late text summarized in even more direct manner the capital importance of this ninth and last *samapatti*: "Venerable monks, achieve the *samapatti* that consists in the cessation of all conscious perception. The *bhikku* who has learned to achieve this has nothing more to do" (*Ciksasamuccaya*, by Santideva, published by Bendall, 1902, p. 48).

THE YOGIS AND THE METAPHYSICIANS

In these *dhyanas* and *samapattis* one will recognize more than one common trait with the various stages of the *samprajnata* and *asamprajnata samadhi* of classical yoga. Moreover, the Buddhists themselves acknowledge that yogis and non-Buddhist ascetics can have access to the four *dhyanas* and the four "gains," and even to the ultimate, the *samapatti* of "unconsciousness" (*asamjnisamapatti*). Except that they challenged the authenticity of this ninth *samapatti* when it was obtained by non-Buddhists: they believed that "the *samapatti* of the destruction of consciousness and sensation" was a discovery of Buddha and represented the establishment of contact with nirvana. Now, if they barred non-Buddhists from access to nirvana, even though agreeing on. the validity of their *jhanas*, it was beyond all doubt because the non-Buddhists did not recognize the *truth* revealed by Buddha. In other words, one could not attain to the unconditional state through mystic meditation alone; one must understand the way that leads to that state, otherwise one was in danger of establishing oneself in some random "heaven" even though thinking that one had attained to nirvana.

This leads us to the problem of gnosis and the "mystic experience," a problem destined to play a fundamental part in the history of Buddhism (but it is major, too, in the whole history of Indian spirituality). The two tendencies—that of the "experimenters" (the *jhains*), if we may thus put it, and that of the "speculatives" (the *dhammayogas*)—are two constants in Buddhism. At a very early stage the canonical texts attempted to establish a harmony between them. A sutra of the Anguttara (III, 355) says: "The monks who dedicate themselves to ecstasy [the *jhayins*] denounce the monks who rely on doctrine [the *dhammayogas*], and the reverse is also true. On the contrary, they ought to respect each other. Rare indeed are those men who spend their lives touching [in other words, 'realizing, experiencing'] the immortal element [*amata dhatu*,

A stupa in Tibet

in other words, nirvana] with their bodies. Rare too are those who see the profound reality [*arthapada*] by penetrating it through *prajna*, through the intelligence." The text emphasizes the extreme difficulty of both "ways": that of gnosis and that of meditative experience. Rare indeed are those who have an *experience* of nirvana; and no less rare are those who "see" reality as it is and who—by means of this intellectual vision—gain deliverance. In the course of time all ways of approaching Buddha on the path of "experience" will become the same: He who learns and understands the Canon assimilates the "doctrinal body" of Buddha; the pilgrim who travels to a stupa containing the relics of the Enlightened One has access to the architectonic mystic body of the same Buddha. But, in the first stage of Buddhism, the problem that arose was the same as that posed in Samkhya and yoga: Between "intelligence" and "experience," which has primacy?

There is proof enough to show that Buddha always closely connected knowledge with a meditative experience of the yogic type. Knowledge was not worth very much to him until it had been "realized" in one's personal experience of it. As for the "meditative experience," it was the "truths" discovered by Buddha that gave it validity. Take the example of the statement: "The body is perishable." It is only by contemplating a corpse that one can assimilate the truth of the statement. But this contemplation of the corpse would lose all its salutary value if it were not based on a truth (*this* body is perishable, *every* body is perishable, there is no salvation except in Buddha's law, etc.) All the truths revealed by Buddha should be experienced in the yogic manner: that is, meditated and experimented.

That is why Ananda, the Master's favorite disciple, even though he had no peer in his erudition (according to the *Theragatha*, verse 1024, he had learned eighty-two thousand *dhammas* from Buddha himself and two thousand from his fellow-disciples), was nevertheless excluded from the council: for he was not *arhat*—that is, he had not had a perfect "yogic experience."

In Ananda the sthavira, who has heard, remembered, recited, and meditated all kinds of sutras, wisdom [*prajna*] is vast, whereas the concentration of thought [*citta samgraha*] is mediocre. But both these qualities must exist together if one is to be able to attain to the state [that consists in] the destruction of impurities [the state of *arhat*] [Nagarjuna's *Mahaprajnaparamitacastra*, Lamotte's translation, *Le Traité de la Grande Vertu de Sagesse*—Volume I, Louvain, 1944, p. 223].

A famous passage of the Samyutta (II, 115) puts Musila and Narada face to face, each representing a certain degree of Buddhist perfection. Both have the same knowledge, but Narada does not regard himself as *arhat*, in the light of the fact that he has not experimentally achieved "contact with nirvana." Here is how he explains himself on the matter: "As if a traveler tortured by thirst found a well in the desert and looked into it; he certainly should have known it to be water, but he would not waste his time touching it with his body. In the same way I have clearly seen 'destruction of existence, nirvana,' but I am not an *arhat*, exempt from vices."

BUDDHA AND THE "MARVELOUS POWERS"

The road to nirvana—exactly like the road to *samadhi* in classical yoga—leads to the possession of the "miraculous powers" (*siddhi; in* Pali, *iddhi*). Now this posed a new problem for Buddha (as it did later for Patanjali); for on the one hand the "powers" were inevitably acquired during the initiation and for this very reason constituted invaluable indications of the monk's spiritual progress, but, on the other hand, they are doubly dangerous because they tempt the monk with a vain "magic mastery of the world" and further threaten to create confusion among the unbelievers. The possession of the *iddhi* is not equivalent to deliverance, but these "marvelous powers" prove in any event that the monk is "deconditioning" himself, that he has suspended the natural laws in whose machinery he

was caught, doomed eternally to endure the determinism of karma. As a consequence the possession of the *iddhi* is not harmful in itself; but the monk should be very careful not to yield to their temptation, and above all he should avoid exhibiting such powers in the presence of the uninitiate. We shall very soon see the reasons invoked by Buddha for prohibiting the employment and display of the *siddhi*.

Let us recall that the "miraculous powers" are part of the five classes of high sciences (*abhijna*, namely: (1) *siddhi*; (2) divine vision; (3) divine hearing; (4) knowledge of the thoughts of others; (5) recollection of former existences). None of these five *abhijna* (*abhinna* in Pali) differs from the "powers" that are available to the non-Buddhist yogi. Even the preliminaries of the meditation that makes it possible to acquire them are similar to those of non-Buddhist yoga: There are matters of mental purity, placidity, etc.

With his heart serene, made pure and translucent, emptied of evil, supple, prepared to act, firm and imperturbable, he (the *bhikku*) applies and inclines his spirit to the modes of the Marvelous Power (*iddhi*). He enjoys the Marvelous Power in its various forms: Being one, he becomes many, being many, he becomes one again; he becomes visible or invisible; without meeting any resistance he goes through a wall, a fortification, a hill, as if each were made of air; he penetrates from top to bottom through solid earth as if it were water; he walks on the water without sinking into it, as if it were solid ground; his legs crossed and bent beneath him, he journeys through the sky like the birds on their wings. Even the moon and the sun, as strong and powerful as they are, he can touch and feel with his hand; remaining in his own body, he reaches even Brahma's heaven. . . . With that clear, celestial ear that surpasses the ear of men, he hears at once human and heavenly sounds, be they distant or close. . . . Penetrating the hearts of others with his own heart, he knows them. . . . With his heart thus serene, etc., he guides and inclines his intelligence toward the knowledge of the memory of his previous existences [Dighanikaya, I, 78 ff.].

Evocation of the *siddhi* in an eighteenth-century Tibetan painting

These lists of the *siddhi* are most often stereotyped, and they are found in all the literature of Indian mystic and ascetic schools. The yogis who were contemporaries of Buddha did not challenge their authenticity, any more than they doubted the genuineness of their yogic ecstasies. But Buddha did not encourage his disciples to strive after the *siddhi:* The only true problem was deliverance, and the possession of the "powers" threatened to distract the monk from his original purpose, nirvana. Reacting against mystic and magic excesses, Buddha did not omit to point out that both the terms and the solution of the problem lay within man as he is. "In truth, my friend, I tell you that in this very body, mortal as it is and only a fathom in height, but conscious and endowed with intelligence, there is the world, as well as its increase and its decline and the road that leads to the transcendence of it" (Anguttara, II, 48; Samyutta, I, 62).

Furthermore the possession of one or another "miraculous power" in no way implemented the propagation of the Buddhist message: Other yogis and ecstatics could perform the same miracles; what is more, one could acquire "powers" by magic without any inner transformation. The unbelieving might think that it was simply a matter of some magic charm.

If a believer [a Buddhist] proclaimed his possession of the mystic powers [*iddhi*], while, being one, he becomes manifold, and, having become manifold, he becomes one again, etc., . . . the unbeliever would say to him: "Well, sir, there is a certain charm called the charm of *gandharva*. It is through its power that he does this!" . . . Well! Kevaddha, it is precisely because I see the peril in the practice of the mystic marvels that I execrate and abhor them and am ashamed of them [Dighanikaya, I, 212 ff.].

That is why Buddha prohibited the display of the *siddhi:* "You must not show the miracles of the *iddhi* to the laity, O *bhikku*, miracles that surpass the power of the common man. He who behaves in such fashion will make himself guilty of an evil deed" (*Vinaya*, II, 212; *Vinaya Texts*, III, 81).

TANTRISM AND YOGA

Among the many meanings of the word *tantra* (from the root *tan*, "to extend, to continue, to multiply"), one in particular concerns us: that of "succession, derivation, continuous process." *Tantra* would be "what broadens knowledge." No one knows for what reason or as a result of what circumstances this word came to designate a major philosophical movement that emerged in the fourth century of the Christian Era and assumed the form of a pan-Indian "mode" beginning in the sixth century. For it was indeed a question of "mode"; suddenly Tantrism enjoyed a tremendous popularity as much among the philosophers and the theologians as among the "communicants" (ascetics, yogis, etc.), and its prestige also reached the "popular" classes. In a relatively short time philosophy, mysticism, ritual, morality, iconography, and literature itself were influenced by Tantrism. It was a pan-Indian movement, for it was assimilated by all the great religions of India and by all the "sectarian" schools. There is an important Buddhist Tantrism and there is also a Hindu Tantrism, but Jainism too accepted certain Tantrist methods (though never that of Tantrism of the "left hand"), and one finds strong Tantrist influences in Kashmiri Sivaism, in the great movement of the Pancatras (about A.D. 550), in the Bhagavata Purana (c. 600), and in other Vishnuist devotional tendencies.

According to Buddhist traditions, Tantrism was supposedly introduced by Asanga (c. 400), the eminent *yogacara* master, and Nagarjuna (second century A.D.), the illustrious representative of *madhyamika* and one of the most celebrated and most mysterious characters in medieval Buddhism; but the problem of the historic origins of Buddhist Tantrism is still far from having been clarified. It is permissible to suppose that the *Vajrayana* ("vehicle of the Diamond"), the name by which

Buddhist Tantrism is generally known, made its appearance at
the beginning of the fourth century and attained its full flight
in the eighth. The *Guhyasamaja tantra*, regarded by some as the
work of Asanga, is probably the most ancient Vajrayanic text,
and undoubtedly one of the most important.

In principle the Buddhist Tantras are divided into four
classes: *kriya tantra*, *carya tantra*, *yoga tantra*, and *anuttara
tantra*. The first two deal with rituals and the last two with the
yogic procedures by means of which one attains to the supreme
verity. Actually almost all the Tantrist texts include ritual directions as well as instructions of a yogic character and philosophical fragments. According to Tibetan tradition, the four
classes of Tantra are supposedly related to the principal human
types and temperaments: The texts of *kriya tantra* are suited to
Brahmans and all others inclined to ritualism, the *carya tantras*
are recommended more for busy men, and so on.

It is worthy of note that Tantrism was developed in India's
two border regions: in the northwest, on the frontier of Af-
ghanistan, and in the eastern part of Bengal and especially in
Assam. Moreover, according to the Tibetan tradition, Nagarjuna
was a native of the region of Andhra, in southern India—in
other words, the very heart of Dravidian India. From this it
might be concluded that, especially in the beginning, Tantrism
developed in the moderately Hinduized provinces where the
spiritual counteroffensive of the aboriginal stocks was at its
height. In fact a great number of foreign, exotic elements
penetrated into Hinduism through the medium of Tantrism;
one finds in it the names and myths of peripheral deities (As-
samese, Burmese, Himalayan, Tibetan, to say nothing of the
Dravidian divinities) and one recognizes exotic rites and be-
liefs. In this respect Tantrism continued and intensified the
process of Hinduization that had begun in the post-Vedic
period; but this time it was a question of assimilating not only
elements of aboriginal India but also elements external to India
properly so-called: the archetype of the "Tantrist country" is
Kamarupa, Assam. One must also reckon with possible gnostic

The *Sakti:* Wife and Mother, divine energy, cosmic force

influences that might have penetrated India, having traveled by way of Iran, on her northwest frontier. In fact more than one puzzling similarity has been observed between Tantrism and the great Western mysteriosophical current that brought together, at the start of the Christian Era, gnosis, hermeticism, Greek-Egyptian alchemy, and the traditions of the Mysteries.

For the first time in the spiritual history of Aryan India the Great Goddess achieved a predominant rank. In the second century of the Christian Era two feminine divinities entered Buddhism: Prajnaparamita, the "creation" of the metaphysicians and the ascetics and the incarnation of Supreme Wisdom, and Tara, the manifestation of the Great Goddess of aboriginal India. In Hinduism the Sakti, the "cosmic force," is elevated to the rank of a Divine Mother who supports the universe and all its living beings as well as the multiple manifestations of the gods. Here, in part, one can recognize that "Mother religion" that once reigned over a huge Aegean-African-Asian area and from the beginning of time was the major form of devotion among India's many autochthonous populations. In this sense the irresistible drive of Tantrism also entailed a new victory for the pre-Aryan popular classes.

But one also perceives in this a kind of religious rediscovery of the mystery of woman, for every woman becomes the incarnation of the Sakti. Mystic emotion in the face of the mystery of conception and fertility, yes; but also recognition of everything in woman that is remote, "transcendent," invulnerable: She becomes the symbol of the irreducibility of the sacred and the divine, the impalpable essence of the ultimate reality. Woman incarnates at once the mystery of the Creation and the mystery of Being, of all that *is* and becomes, dies and is reborn in a manner beyond understanding. On the metaphysical as well as the mythological plane this is an extension of the schema of the philosophy of Samkhya: The Spirit, the "male," the *purusha*, is the "great impotent," the Immobile, the contemplative; it is *prakrti* that labors, engenders, and nourishes. When a great danger threatens the foundations of the cosmos, the gods call on the Sakti to drive it away.

One must never lose sight of this primacy of the Sakti—in the final instance, the Divine Wife and Mother—in Tantrism and all the movements that derive from it. This was the road by which the great subterranean current of autochthonous, popular spirituality emerged into Hinduism. Philosophically, the rediscovery of the goddess is bound up with the carnal condition of the spirit in *kali yuga*. Indeed the authors present the Tantrist doctrine as a new revelation of the timeless truth intended for the man of that "dark age" in which the spirit is thickly veiled by the flesh. The doctors of Hindu Tantrism regarded the Vedas and the Brahman tradition as inadequate to "modern times": man no longer enjoyed the spiritual spontaneity and vigor that he possessed at the beginning of the cycle, he was incapable of acceding directly to Truth (*Maha-nirvana-tantra*, I, 20–29, 37–50); he must therefore "go back to the source" and, to that end, start from the fundamental, specific experiences of his blighted condition—in other words, the very sources of his life. That is why the "living rite" plays a decisive part in the Tantrist *sadhana*; that is why the "heart" and "sexuality" serve as vehicles for accession to transcendence.

For Buddhists too the *Vajrayana* represents a new revelation of Buddha's doctrine adapted to the much diminished capacities of modern man. In the *Kalacakra Tantra* we are told how King Sucandra, approaching Buddha, asked him for the yoga that would save men from *kali yuga*. Thereupon Buddha disclosed to him that the cosmos was to be found in the very body of man; he explained to him the importance of sexuality, and he taught him to control temporal rhythms through respiratory disciplines in order to elude the grip of time. The flesh, the living cosmos, and time constitute three basic elements in the Tantrist *sadhana*.

This is the source of a primary characteristic of Tantrism: its anti-ascetic and, in general, anti-speculative attitude. "Donkeys and other animals too walk about naked. Does that make them yogis?" (*Kularnava Tantra*, V, 48). Inasmuch as the body represents the cosmos and all the gods, and inasmuch as deliverance can be attained only by starting from the body, it is important to have a strong, healthy body. In certain Tantrist schools contempt for asceticism and speculation is accompanied by the complete rejection of all meditative practices: Deliverance is pure spontaneity. Saraha wrote: "The childish yogis, like so many other ascetics, will never be capable of finding their own nature. There is no need of *mantras* or images or *dharanis*: all are sources of confusion. In vain is deliverance sought through meditation. . . . Everyone is hypnotized by the *jhana* system (meditation), but no one is interested in achieving his own Self." Another *sahajiya* author, Lui-pa, wrote: "What is the good of meditation? In spite of meditation one dies in anguish. Abandon all complicated practices and the hope of acquiring *siddhi*, and accept the "void" (*sunya*) as your true nature."

Viewed from without, then, Tantrism would seem to represent an "easy way" that leads pleasantly and almost without obstacles to freedom. For the Tantrists of the "left hand" (*vamacari*) thought that they could arrive at identification with Siva and Sakti by employing wine, meat, and carnal love as ritual instruments. The *Kularnava Tantra* (VIII, 107 ff.) stipulates indeed that the supreme union with God can be obtained only through sexual union. And the famous *Guhyasamaja Tantra* summarily states: "No one succeeds in gaining perfection by means of difficult and wearying exercises; but perfection can be easily won by means of satisfying all one's desires" (Bhattacharyya edition, Baroda, 1931, p. 27).

But the "easiness" of the Tantrist path is more apparent than real. In fact the Tantrist path presupposes a long and arduous *sadhana* that is at times reminiscent of the alchemists' *opus*. The "void" (*sunya*) is not merely a "non-being"; rather, it is similar to the Vedanta's *brahman*, it is adamantine in essence, and that is why it is called *vajra* ("diamond"). "*Sunyata*, which is firm, substantial, indivisible, and impenetrable, immune to fire and imperishable, is called *vajra*" (*Advaya-vajra-samgraha*, Gaekwar Oriental Series, p. 37). Now the ideal of the Buddhist *Tantrika* is to transform himself into a "being of diamond," in

which, on the one hand, his ideal is that of the Indian alchemist
and the Hathayogi, and, on the other hand, it recalls the famous
equation of the Upanishads: *atman equals brahman.* In Tantrist metaphysics, both Hindu and Buddhist, absolute reality,
the *Urgrund*, contains in itself all dualities and polarities, reunited, reincorporated in a state of absolute unity (*advaya*).
The Creation and the process of becoming that derives from it
represent the explosion of the primordial unity and the separation of the two principles (*Siva-Sakti*, etc.); consequently one
experiences a state of duality (object-subject, etc.)—and this is
suffering, illusion, "enslavement." The goal of Tantrist *sadhana*
is the reunion of the two polar principles in the disciple's soul
and body. "Revealed" through the knowledge of *kali yuga*,
Tantrism is above all a practice, an action, a realization
(*sadhana*). But, although the revelation is intended for everyone, the Tantrist path entails an initiation that can be given
only by a *guru*; whence the importance of the master, who
alone, "from lip to ear," can transmit the secret, esoteric doctrine. In this respect too Tantrism offers striking analogies with
the mysteries of antiquity and the various forms of gnosis.

TANTRIST "REALIZATION": DIVINE IMAGES AND MYSTIC SOUNDS

Tantrist *sadhana* includes a certain number of meditative
rituals and exercises that can be accomplished only with the
help of yogic practices. One cannot "visualize" a divine image
—that is, construct it mentally and project it on to a kind of
inner screen—without having mastered *dharana* and *dhyana*.
The visualization of a divine image is followed by a more difficult exercise: identification with the divinity that it represents.
A Tantrist maxim points out that "one cannot adore a god
unless one is oneself a god." To identify oneself with the
divinity, to become a god oneself, means to awaken the divine
forces that slumber in man.

In a certain measure it is iconography—for in the beginning
it was necessary to imitate Buddha's postures and movements—

on which the *mudras* are dependent. This term has a multiplicity of meanings (seal, gesture, arrangement of the fingers, etc.),
one of which is erotic (cf. M. Eliade, *Le Yoga*, pp. 250 ff.).

Tantrism has elevated the "mystic syllables"—*mantra* and
dharani—to the dignity of a means of salvation (*mantra yana*).
It is important to distinguish various aspects in this universal
vogue of the sacred formula, a vogue that has culminated on the
one hand in the loftiest speculations on "mystic sounds" and,
on the other, in the prayer mill of the Lamas. The practical
value and philosophical importance of *mantras* are derived from
sources of two kinds: first of all there is the yogic function of
phonemes employed as "supports" for concentration; then
there is the uniquely Tantrist contribution: the elaboration of
a gnostic system and an internalized liturgy.

Earlier, in the Vedic period, *dharani*, "that which upholds or
encloses," served as a "support" and a "defense" for concentration (*dharana*). The *dharanis*, like the *mantras*, are learned
from the lips of the master. Therefore there is no question of
phonemes taken from profane language or susceptible of being
learned from books: They must be "received." Once received
from the lips of the master, however, the *mantras* possess unlimited powers. The reason is that they *are* (or at any rate they
can become, through the use of the proper recitation) the
"objects" that they represent. Each god, each degree of sanctity,
for example, possesses a *bija mantra*, a "mystic sound" that is
its "seed," its "support"—in other words, its very *being*. By
repeating this *bija mantra* in conformance with the rules, the
practitioner appropriates its ontological essence to himself, assimilates the god, the state of sanctity, etc., into himself in a
concrete, immediate fashion. There is an occult "correspondence" between the "mystic" letters and syllables and the subtle
organs of the human body, on the one hand, and these organs
and the divine forces asleep or manifested in the cosmos, on the
other hand. By working on a symbol, one "awakens" all the
forces that correspond to it at all levels of being. Between the
mantrayana and iconography, for instance, there is perfect cor-

The Tibetan prayer mill and chaplet, the instruments
repetition of the mystic phrases

The *mantras* learned from the master's lips

respondence; for there are a special letter, color, and image to correspond to each plane and each degree of sanctity. (On the similarities between yogic-Tantrist techniques and Moslem *dhikr*, see L. Gardet, *La mention du nom divin (dhikr) dans la mystique indienne*, and M. Eliade, *Le Yoga*, pp. 220 ff.)

HATHAYOGA AND THE DISCOVERY OF THE BODY

In Tantrism the human body acquired an importance without precedent in India's spiritual history. The body is no longer the "source of sufferings" but the surest and most accomplished instrument available to man for the "conquest of death." One can distinguish two different but convergent orientations in this emphatic evaluation of the human body and its possibilities: (1) the importance ascribed to the *total experience of life* as forming an integral part of *sadhana*, and this is the general position of all schools of Tantrism; (2) the determination to master the body in order to transmute it into a "divine body," and this is above all the position taken by Hathayoga.

The appearance of Hathayoga is linked with the name of an ascetic, Gorakhnath, who founded an order called the Kanphata Yogis. He is supposed to have lived during the twelfth century or perhaps even earlier. All that we know about Gorakhnath is distorted by a sectarian mythology and a rich magic folklore; but there are reasonably sure grounds to suppose that he maintained close relations with *Vajrayana*. In addition, the Hathayogic manuscripts refer to sexual practices specified by Buddhist Tantrism. Gorakhnath is credited with the authorship of a treatise, *Hathayoga*, which has since been lost, and a text that has been preserved, the *Goraksasataka*. The Kanphatas called their own discipline Hathayoga, but this word was soon expanded to cover all the traditional prescriptions and disciplines by means of which perfect mastery of the body was to be obtained. In any case, the Hathayogic texts derive in one way or another from the literature, or what is supposed to be such, of the Gorakhna-

thayogis. There is a rather large number of these texts, but, apart from the *Goraksasataka*, only three are of any interest: (1) *Hathayogapradipika* (by Svatmarama Svamin, probably fifteenth century); (2) *Gheranda samhita* (by one Gheranda, a *vaisnava* of Bengal), which largely repeats the *Hathayogapradipika*; (3) *Siva samhita* (longer than the others—it contains 517 stanzas —and philosophically more highly developed; Tantrist Yoga is strongly colored by the Vedanta). The oldest of these three texts would appear to be the *Hathayogapradipika*, based according to tradition on the now lost *Hathayoga*.

The influences of Buddhism are easily identifiable. The Vedanta is mingled with yoga, but philosophical justification has a very minor place in these summary writings devoted almost wholly to technical prescriptions. The states of consciousness corresponding to the various exercises are mentioned only rarely, and in a rudimentary fashion. It is chiefly the physics and physiology of meditation that concern the authors, who emphasize their magic and hygienic virtues. Like refrains, "eliminates old age and death" and "conquers death" recur to illustrate the true meaning and ultimate orientation of all these techniques.

Hathayoga attributes great importance to the preliminary "purifications," of which it distinguishes six kinds: *dhauti, basti, neti, nauli, trataka,* and *kapala bhati.* The most common were the first two. The *dhauti* (literally, "cleansings") were divided into a number of classes and subclasses: "internal cleansings," cleansings of the teeth, the rectum, etc. The most efficacious was *dhauti karma*: one swallows a bit of fabric and leaves it in the stomach for a period (see also Theos Bernard, *Hatha Yoga,* pp. 15 ff.). *Basti* entails the cleansing of the large intestine and the rectum, which is accomplished by using an anal pump. *Neti* consists in cleansing the nasal cavities by means of wires introduced into the nostrils. Vigorous, complex movements of the stomach and the intestines are employed in the practice of *nauli,* an exercise called *lauliki yoga* (cf. Bernard's experiments, pp. 21 ff.) by the *Gheranda samhita* (I, 52). *Trataka* consists in focusing the eyes on a small object until tears are produced.

Nauli: the contraction of a muscular area of the abdomen in order to exert direct action on the functioning of the digestive apparatus

Kapala bhati includes three variants of "purification" of the nasal cavities: Water is inhaled through the nostrils and spat out through the mouth, etc.

The texts point out emphatically that these "purifications" are of very great importance to the yogi's health, that they prevent liver and stomach diseases, etc. There is no lack of specific indications of diet, social behavior (the yogi must avoid travel, morning baths, the company of women, and evil men). As was to be expected, "practice" (*abhyasa*) plays a decisive part: nothing can be achieved without "practice," which, furthermore, is a Tantrist leitmotiv. In addition, if one "realizes" Hathayoga, there exists no crime or sin that cannot be erased (killing a Brahman or a foetus, violating the bed of one's spiritual master, etc.—all crimes that are abolished by the *yonimudra*; cf. *Gher. samh.*, III, 43–44). Homage to the magic efficacity of an act perfectly performed is as ancient as India.

Pranayama destroys sins and confers the eighty-four *siddhis*, but this exercise serves above all to purify the *nadis*. Each new step in the respiratory discipline is accompanied by physiological phenomena. In general the duration of sleep, defecation, and urine are reduced. During the first stage of *pranayama* the yogi's body begins to perspire (*HY-Pr.*, 12–13; *Siva Sam.*, III, 40); during the second stage he begins to tremble; during the third "he starts to hop like a frog," and in the fourth he rises into the air (*Siva Sam.*, III, 41; cf. *Gher. Sam.*, V, 45–57). According to Theos Bernard's personal experiments (*op. cit.*, p. 32), all these symptoms except the last correspond to states really experienced during the practice of Hathayogic *pranayama*. These, however, are symptoms of only minor importance, recorded in the texts only because they can be used for objective verification of the success of the practice.

The real "powers" acquired by the yogis, on the other hand, are much more important, especially their amazing ability to control the neurovegetative system and the influence that they can exert on their cardiac and respiratory rhythms. We shall not discuss this important matter here. It is sufficient to point out that, according to Drs. Charles Laubry and Thérèse Brosse, the Hathayogis extend to the smooth fibers the normal control of the striated fibers. This would explain the intake and expulsion of fluids by the urethra or the rectum, as well as the withholding of seminal emission (and even the "return of the semen"), a practice of the first importance in "left-handed" Tantrism (cf. *Le Yoga,* pp. 236 ff.).

THE SUBTLE ORGANS AND MYSTIC PHYSIOLOGY

The body—physical and "subtle" at the same time—is supposed to be composed of a certain number of *nadis* (literally, canals, veins, or arteries, but also nerves) and *cakras* (literally, circles, discs, but usually translated as "centers"). With some simplification it might be said that vital energy in the form of "airs" circulates through the *nadis* and that cosmic and divine energy lies latent in the *cakras.*

There is a considerable number of *nadis,* but seventy-two among them have special importance. Those that play the major part in the yogic techniques are *ida, pingala,* and *susumna;* they issue, respectively, in the left nostril, the right nostril, and the *brahmarandhra (sutura frontalis).* The description of the *nadis* is most frequently brief: Stock phrases and stereotyped expressions are numerous, and the "secret language" in which many Tantrist texts are written makes understanding even more difficult. (On this "secret language," cf. *Le Yoga,* pp. 251 ff., 394.) According to Hathayoga, the *nadis* have become "impure" and are "obstructed" in the uninitiate; they must be "purified" through yogic practice (*asana, pranayama,* etc.). The *ida* and the *pingala* carry the two "airs"—*prana* and *apana*—but also all the body's subtle energy. As for the *susumna,* this central channel plays an essential part in what is called the "awakening" of the *kundalini* and the journey through the six "centers" (*cakras*). In fact, the *kundalini*—the cosmic energy that exists in everyone—is described in the guise of a serpent coiled at the base of the spinal column in the *muladharacakra*

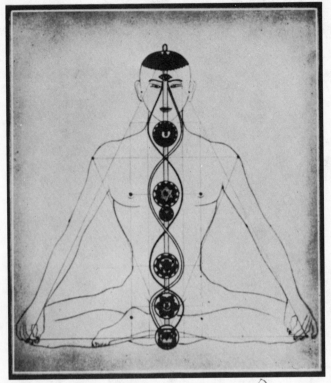

The six *cakras* and the ascent of the *kundalini*
to the upper lotus

(sacrococcygeal plexus). As a result of certain yogic exercises
the *kundalini* is "awakened" and ascends through the *susumna*
to the top of the head. During its journey the *kundalini* passes
successively through the *svadhisthana cakra* (situated in the
sacral area), the *manipura cakra* (epigastric plexus), the *ana-
hata cakra* (the area of the heart), the *visuddha cakra* (laryngeal
and pharyngeal region), and the *ajna cakra* (situated between
the eyebrows, in the hollow area), and arrives at the *sahasrara
cakra*, also called the *brahmandhra* (the top of the head). It is
there that final union is achieved between Siva and Sakti: the
goal of Tantrist *sadhana*.

The awakening of the *kundalini* produces extremely intense heat, and its progression through the *cakras* is evidenced by the fact that the lower part of the body becomes inert and frigid, like a corpse, while the part traversed by the *kundalini* is burning. The act of awakening itself is instigated by a technique the essential element of which consists in stopping respiration (*kumbhaka*) through a special bodily position (*asana, mudra*). In order to hasten the ascent of the *kundalini*, certain Tantrist schools have combined the positions of the body with sexual practices. The underlying idea is that it was necessary to achieve the simultaneous "immobility" of breath, thought, and semen (cf. the texts cited in *Le Yoga*, pp. 250 ff., 253 ff.). But it must not be forgotten that one is in a universe of analogies, homologies, and double meanings. Every erotic phenomenon can express a Hathayogic exercise or a stage in meditation, just as any symbol, any "state of sanctity" may be colored by an erotic meaning.

Ritual sexual union (*maithuna*) seeks above all the integration of the polar principles: "True sexual union is the union of the *Parasakti* (*kundalini*) with *Atman*; the others represent only carnal relations with women" (*Kularnava Tantra*, V, 111, 112). *Maithuna* ought never to be consummated by the ejaculation of semen (cf. *Le Yoga*, pp. 256 ff.). Otherwise the yogi will fall under the law of time and death like any common wencher. In these practices "sensual delight" fulfills the function of a "means," for it procures the maximal tension that abolishes normal consciousness and inaugurates the state of nirvana, the paradoxical experience of nonduality. The conjunction of opposing principles (Siva and Sakti, etc.) represents the transcendence of the world of phenomena, the abolition of all experience of duality.

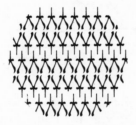

Conclusion

Yoga constitutes *a specific dimension of the Indian spirit*, to such a degree that, wherever Indian culture and religion have penetrated, one finds also a more or less pure form of yoga. In India itself yoga has been incorporated and given value by all religious movements, whether Hinduist or "heretical." The various syncretist yogas of modern India constitute further proof that Indian religious experience requires the yogic methods of "meditation" and "concentration" as necessities. For in the end yoga has absorbed and incorporated all kinds of spiritual and mystic techniques from the most rudimentary to the most complex. The generic term, yogi, designates the saint and the mystic as well as the magician, the orgiast, and the common fakir and sorcerer. Each of these types of magic-religious behavior, moreover, corresponds to a specific form of yoga.

The yogi of Mahavalipuram

In order to become what it has been for many centuries—
that is, a pan-Indian corpus of spiritual techniques—yoga must
have abundantly answered the deepest needs of the Indian soul.
We have seen how it responded to them: From the beginning
yoga has accented reaction against metaphysical speculations
and the excesses of a fossilized ritualism; it represented the same
tendency toward the concrete, toward personal experience, that
is found in the popular devotion expressed in *puja* and *bhakti.*
One always finds a form of yoga whenever there is question of
experiencing the sacred or arriving at complete *mastery of oneself,* which is itself the first step toward the magic mastery of the
world. It is a highly significant fact that the noblest mystic experiences as well as the boldest magic desires are accomplished
through yogic technique, or, more precisely, that yoga can adapt
itself equally to the one or the other path. Many hypotheses
might prove its validity. The first would call on the two spiritual
traditions that finally constituted Hinduism after many tensions
and a long labor of synthesis: the religious tradition of the
Aryan-language Indo-Europeans and the tradition of the aborigines (quite complex and including Dravidian, Mundan, Proto-
Mundan, and Harappan elements). The Indo-Europeans con-
tributed a society of patriarchal structure, a pastoral economy,
and the worship of the gods of the sky and the atmosphere—
in a word, the "religion of the Father." The pre-Aryans already
knew agriculture and urbanism (the Indus civilization), and, in
general, they shared the "religion of the Mother." Hinduism as
it has existed since the end of the Middle Ages represents the
synthesis of these two traditions, but with the marked predominance of the aboriginal factors: The contribution of the
Indo-Europeans, in the end, has been radically Asianized. Hinduism signifies the religious victory of the soil.

Although the magic conception of the world is more ac-
centuated among the Indo-Europeans, one would hesitate to
ascribe to them the magic tendency evidenced in the yoga
complex or to credit the mystic tendency exclusively to the
aborigines. It seems to me more justified to attribute the con-

siderable importance of ritualism, and the speculations to which
it has given rise, to the Indo-European contribution and to
credit the aborigines with the tendency toward the concrete in
religious experience and the necessity for a mystic devotion with
respect to personal or local divinities (*istadevata, gramadevata*).
To the extent to which it represents a reaction against ritualism
and scholastic speculations, yoga shares the aboriginal tradition
and is opposed to the Indo-European religious heritage. But
yoga cannot simply be ranked among the innumerable varieties
of primitive mysticism that are customarily designated by the
name of shamanism. Yoga is not a technique of ecstasy; on the
contrary, it makes every effort to achieve absolute concentration
in order to attain to enstasis.

We have directed attention to the yogic symbolism of death
and rebirth: death to the profane human condition, rebirth to
a transcendent modality. The yogi endeavors totally to "reverse" normal behavior: he imposes on himself a petrified immobility of the body (*asana*), the cadencing and suspension of
respiration (*pranayama*), the fixation of the psychomental flow
(*ekagrata*), the immobility of thought, the "stoppage" of the
semen. On all levels of human experience he does the *opposite*
of what life calls on him to do. Now the symbolism of the
"opposite" alludes at the same time to the condition post
mortem and to the divine condition: It is known that the right
on earth corresponds to the left in the beyond, a broken vase
here corresponds to an unbroken vase in the world of the grave
and the gods, etc. The "reversal" of normal behavior places the
yogi outside life. But he does not stop halfway: Death is followed by an initiatory rebirth. The yogi makes a "new body"
for himself just as the neophyte in primitive societies was supposed to obtain a new body through his initiation.

At first glance the *rejection of life* required by yoga might
seem frightening, for it entails more than a funereal symbolism:
experiences that are so many anticipations of death. The arduous, complicated procedure of detachment and final elimination
of all contents that belong to the psychophysiological levels of

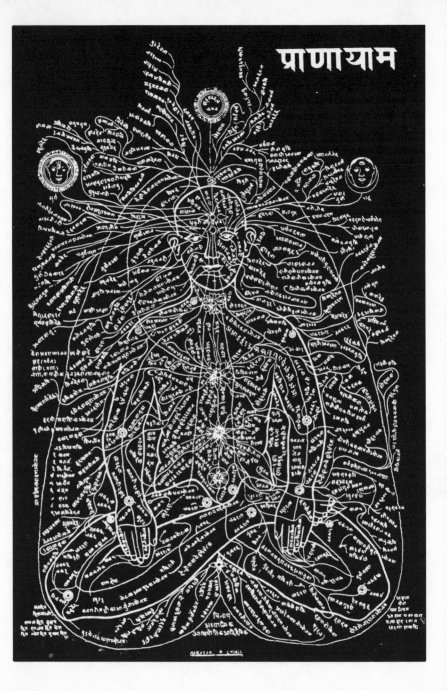

human experience: Is this not a reminder of the process of death? To India, in actuality, death is made manifest by the brutal separation of the spirit from all psychophysiological experiences. And, on closer examination, the mystery of deliverance, the regression of the elements (*tattva*) toward *prakrti*, also signifies an anticipation of death. Certain yogic-Tantrist exercises are merely an "anticipated visualization" of the decomposition of the elements and their return into the circuit of nature, a phenomenon normally initiated by death. Many of the experiences beyond the grave described in the *Bardo Thödol*, the *Tibetan Book of the Dead*, are strangely like the yogic-Tantrist meditative exercises.

We know now that this anticipatory death is an initiatory death—in other words, that it is necessarily followed by a rebirth. It is with a view to this rebirth to another way of being that the yogi offers the sacrifice of everything that seems important on the plane of profane existence. Not only the sacrifice of his "life" but also that of his "personality." From the point of view of a profane existence this sacrifice becomes incomprehensible. But we know the reply of Indian philosophy: The point of view of profane existence is distorted. And there are two reasons why this is so: (1) life without sanctity is suffering and illusion, and (2) it would be impossible to resolve any ultimate problem from the point of view of this life. Let us recall the reply given by Samkhya and yoga to the problems relative to the cause and inception of the pseudoenslavement of the spirit in the circuit of matter and life: These problems are insoluble in the present human condition; in other words, they are "mysteries" to every intelligence that has not been delivered (we would say "to every fallen intelligence"). If one wishes to attain to understanding of these "mysteries," one must raise oneself to another mode of being and, in order to do so, it is necessary to "die" to this life and to "sacrifice" the personality born of temporality and created by history (since personality is first of all the memory of our own history). The ideal of yoga, the state of *jivanmukta*, is to live in an "eternal present," out-

Matter, life, spirit . . .

side time. "The man liberated in life" no longer possesses a personal consciousness—that is, nourished on his own history—but a witnessing consciousness, which is pure lucidity and spontaneity. I shall not attempt to describe this paradoxical state: Gained through "death" to the human condition and rebirth into a transcendent mode of being, it is also impossible of reduction to our categories. Let us nevertheless emphasize one thing of primarily historical interest: Yoga repeats and extends the immemorial symbolism of initiation; in other words, it incorporates into itself a universal tradition of the religious history of mankind: the anticipation of death in order to be assured of rebirth into a sanctified life—that is, a life made *real* by the incorporation of the sacred. But India has gone especially far on this traditional plane. To yoga the initiatory rebirth means the procurement of immortality or absolute freedom. It is in the very structure of this paradoxical state, which lies beyond profane existence, that one should seek the explanation of the coexistence of "magic" and "mysticism" in yoga: Everything is a function of the meaning that is ascribed to *freedom*.

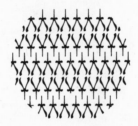

Chronology

c. 2700–1700 B.C.	Indus civilization (Harappa, Mohenjo-Daro).
c. 1500–1200	Aryan invasion of India. Composition of the most ancient hymns of the Rig Veda.
c. 1200–900	Composition of the Rig Veda.
c. 900–500	Period of the later Vedas, the Brahmanas, and the first Upanishads.
c. 800	Aryans infiltrate into eastern Bihar and Bengal.
c. 600	End of the Brahmana period.
c. 563–483 or 558–478	Siddharta Gautama, the Buddha.
480	First Buddhist council at Rajagriha.
327–325	Invasion of India by Alexander the Great.

Fourth century B.C.–fourth century A.D.	Composition of the religious and didactic sections of the Mahabharata.
c. 300	Megasthenes, Greek ambassador from Seleucus Nicator, visits the court of King Chandragupta.
269–232	Asoka.
200 B.C.–A.D. 200	Period of strongest Buddhist and Jain influence.
190	The Greek kingdoms in northwest India.
170–165	The Yue-tche (Iranians) invade northwest India.
c. 150	Milinda (Greek: Menander), the most illustrious of the Indo-Greek kings.
Second century B.C.	Patanjali the grammarian (identified by some with the author of the *Yoga Sutras*).
100 B.C.–A.D. 100	Composition of the Bhagavad-Gita.
Second century B.C.–fourth century A.D.	Possible dates of composition of *Yoga Sutras*.
100 B.C.–A.D. 200	Development of *mahayana* Buddhism.
Third-fourth centuries A.D.	Isvara Krishna writes *Samkhya-Karika*.
400–500	Foundation of the great Buddhist monastery of Nalanda.
405	Fa-hsien, the Chinese pilgrim, arrives in Magadha.
454	First invasion of India by the Huns.
495	Second invasion by the Huns.
629–645	Sojourn of Hiuan-tsang, a Chinese pilgrim, in India.
Seventh–eighth centuries	Vyasa writes a commentary, *Yogabhashya*, on Patanjali's *Yoga Sutras*.
Seventh–ninth centuries	Probable composition of the first Tantrist treatises.
600–700	Bhagavata Purana.
711–715	Muhammad ibn Qasim conquers Sindi.
c. 750	Padma Sambhava introduces esoteric Tantrism into Tibet.
788–820	Traditional dates of Sankara.

Ninth century	Vacaspati Misra writes *Tattvavaisaradi* (commentary on *Yoga Sutras*) and *Samkhya-tattvakaumudi*.
c. 1000	King Bhoja writes his commentary, *Rajamartanda*.
999–1026	Mahmud of Ghaznim ravages India.
c. 1025	Albiruni (973–1048) translates a large part of *Yoga Sutras* into Arabic (*Kitab Patanjala*).
Twelfth century	Gorakhnath, founder of the order of the Kanphata Yogis, author of lost treatise, *Hathayoga*, and of *Gorakshasataka*.
1137	Death of Ramanuja.
1192	Crushing Moslem victory. Buddhism disappears as an organized religion.
1197	Monastery of Nalanda destroyed by Moslems.
c. fourteenth century	*Samkhya Sutra*.
Fifteenth century	Aniruddha writes his commentary, *Samkhya-Sutravrtti*.
Sixteenth century	Vijnana Bhikshu writes *Samkhya-pravacana-bhashya* (commentary on *Samkhya Sutra*), *Yoga-varttika* (commentary on Vyasa's *Yoga-bhashya*), and *Yoga-sara-samgraha*, a brief treatise on Patanjali's doctrine.
	Ramananda Sarasvati writes *Manibrabha* (commentary on *Yoga Sutras*).
	Prunandasvamin's *Shatcakranirupana* (the most precise description of the *cakras* and of the Tantrist initiation).
1834–1886	Sri Ramakrishna.
1862–1902	Swami Vivekananda
1872–1950	Sri Audobindo.

YOGA APHORISMS

OF

PATANJALI.

INTRODUCTION.

---

a. Salutation to Ganesa! May that union of the twin-persons of Siva and his spouse,—by the recollection of which one enjoys emancipation, hard as it is to attain,—produce for you all blessings!*

b. From such passages of scripture as this—viz.—" NÁCHIKETA having received this science [viz. the Vedánta] declared to him by Yama, and all the rules of the *yoga,* having arrived at the Supreme Soul, became passionless and immortal :—whosoever else also thus knows the Supreme Spirit, &c.,"—it is inferred that the rules of the *yoga* ought to be understood and practised by those who are desirous of emancipation. Therefore the venerable PA-TANJALI, being about to exhibit the rules of the *yoga,* in order to gain the attention of his disciples, states as follows what doctrine it is that is going to be entered upon.†

---

* श्री गणेशाय नमः। देहाद्वैयोगशिवयोस्त्र श्रेयांसि तनोतु वः। दुष्प्रापमपि यत्स्मृत्या जनः कैवल्यमश्नुते॥

† मृत्युप्रोक्तां नाचिकेतो ऽय लब्ध्वा विद्यामेतां योगवि-धिच्चकृत्स्नं ब्रह्मप्राप्तो विरजो ऽभद्विमृत्युरन्यो ऽप्येवं यो वेत्ता

A

Bilingual edition, Allahabad, 1852

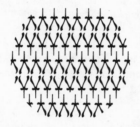

Bibliography

SAMKHYA TEXTS:

Krishna, Isvara, *Samkhya Karika* (*S.K.*). The best edition is that of S. S. Suryanarayana Sastri, University of Madras, 1930, with introduction, English translation, and notes.

Misra, Vacaspati, *Samkhya-tattva-kaumudi*. Sanskrit text and English translation by Ganganath Jha, Bombay, 1896; German translation by R. Garbe, Munich, 1892.

Samkhya-pravacana-Sutra (*S.S.*), attributed by tradition to Kapila: its probable date is the fourteenth century. Commentaries by Aniruddha, fourteenth century, edited and translated into English by R. Garbe, Calcutta, 1888–1892; and by Vijnana Bhikshu, fourteenth century, edited by R. Garbe, Harvard, 1895; German translation by Garbe, Leipzig, 1889; English translation by Nandalal Sinha, Allahabad, 1915.

On Samkhya, see R. Garbe, *Samkhya und Yoga*, Strasbourg, 1896;
A. B. Keith, *The Samkhya System*, second edition, Calcutta,
1924. Bibliography in M. Eliade, *Le Yoga*, Paris, 1954, pp.
360–363.

PATANJALI AND THE TEXTS OF CLASSICAL YOGA:

The most up-to-date edition of the *Yoga Sutras* (*Y.S.*), with
Vyasa's commentary and Vacaspati Misra's gloss, is that published
by Anandashrama Sanskrit Series, No. 47. These texts have been
translated into English by J. H. Woods, *The Yoga System of
Patanjali*, Cambridge, Mass., 1924, Harvard Oriental Series, XVII;
and by Rama Prasada, *Patanjali's Yoga Sutras, with the Commentary of Vyasa and the Gloss of Vacaspati Misra*, Allahabad,
1910 (third edition, 1924).

Bhikshu Vijnana, (sixteenth century), wrote a commentary on
     Vyasa's *Yoga-bhashya: Yogavarttika*, published by "The Pandit,"
     New Series, Vols. V–VI, Benares, 1883–1884. Also *Yoga-sara-
     samgraha* (a brief treatise on Patanjali's doctrine), edited in an
     English version by Ganganath Jha, Bombay, 1894.
Bhoja King, (beginning of eleventh century), wrote the commentary
     Raja-martanda on the *Yoga Sutras* (edited in English version by
     Rajendralala Mitra, Calcutta, 1883).
Daniélou, Alain, *Yoga, Méthode de réintégration*, Paris, 1951.
Dasgupta, S. N., *A Study of Patanjali*, Calcutta, 1920; *Yoga as
     Philosophy and Religion*, London, 1924; *Yoga Philosophy in
     Relation to Other Systems of Indian Thought*, Calcutta, 1930;
     A History of Indian Philosophy, I, Cambridge, 1922, pp. 226 ff.
Eliade, Mircea, *Yoga—Essai sur les origines de la mystique indienne*,
     Paris-Bucharest, 1936; *Techniques du Yoga*, Paris, 1948; *Le
     Yoga, Immortalité et Liberté*, Paris, 1954 (corrected and much
     enlarged edition of the 1936 *Essai*; except for a few paragraphs,
     the entire book has been rewritten).
Hauer, J. W., *Die Anfänge der Yoga-praxis*, Stuttgart, 1922; *Die
     Yoga als Heilweg*, Stuttgart, 1932; *Die Yoga: ein indischer Weg
     zum Selbst*, Stuttgart, 1958.
Jha, Ganganath, *The Yoga-Darshana* (second edition, Madras,
     1934): contains the translation of the *Yoga Sutras* with Vyasa's
     commentary.

Masson-Oursel, P., *Le Yoga* (*Que sais-je?* series), Paris, 1954.

Radhakrisnan, S., *Indian Philosophy*, II, London, 1927, pp. 336 ff.

Sarasvati Ramananda, (sixteenth century), *Maniprabha*, a commentary on the *Yoga Sutras*, translated by J. H. Woods, in *Journal of American Oriental Society*, XXXIV, 1914, pp. 1–114. On the chronology of the Samkhya and Yoga texts, cf. M. Eliade, *Le Yoga, Immortalité et Liberté*, Paris, 1954, pp. 360–364.

Yoga, Science de l'homme intégral, texts and studies published under the direction of Jacques Masui, Paris, 1953.

ON HATHAYOGA:

Gheranda, *Gheranda-samhita*, edited by Bhuvanana Chandra Vasaka, Calcutta, 1877; English translation by Rai Bahadur Sris Chandra Vasu, Bombay, 1895, reissued Allahabad, 1914, in *Sacred Books of the Hindus*, and Adyar, 1933; German translation by R. Schmidt, *Fakire und Fakirtum im alten und modernen India*, Berlin, 1908 (second edition, 1921).

Siva Samhita, edited in English translation by Rai Bahadur Sris Chandra Vasu, Lahore, 1888, reprinted Allahabad, 1914.

(Many extracts from these three works will be found in Theos Bernard, *Hatha Yoga*, New York, 1944, and Alain Daniélou, *Yoga, Méthode de réintégration*, Paris, 1951.)

Swamin, Svatmarama, *Hathayogapradipika* (probably fifteenth century): edition with commentary of Brahmananda and glosses by Sridhara, Bombay, 1889 (several printings); German translation annotated by Hermann Walter, Munich, 1893; English edition translated by Brahmananda Bhaba, Bombay, 1889; Srinivasa Iyangar, Bombay, 1893 (latest printing, Adyar, Madras, 1933); Pancam Sinh, Allahabad, 1915, in the series *Sacred Books of the Hindus*.

Scientific observations on the Hathayogis: Charles Laubry and Thérèse Brosse, "Documents recueillis aux Indes sur les "Yoguis" par l'enregistrement simultané du pouls, de la respiration et de l'électrocardiagramme," in *la Presse médicale*, No. 83, October 14, 1936. See also Hubert Risch, *Le Hatha Yoga: Exposé sommaire de la méthode, quelques expériences physiologiques et applications thérapeutiques*, (thesis, Faculté de Médecine, Paris, 1951); Dr. Jean Filliozat, "Les limites des pouvoirs humains dans l'Inde," in *Limites de l'Humain*, *Études Carmélitaines*, 1953, pp. 23–38.

ON BUDDHISM AND YOGA:

Conze, Edward, *Buddhism*, Oxford, 1951, pp. 161 ff.
Eliade, M., *Le Yoga*, etc., *op. cit.*, pp. 169–204, 382–383.
Lamotte, Étienne, *Le Traité de la Grande Vertu de Sagesse de Nagarjuna* (*Mahaprajnaparamitrasastra*), Louvain, 1944, 1949, 2 vols.
La Vallée-Poussin, Louis de, "Le Bouddhisme et le Yoga de Patanjali," in *Mélanges chinois et bouddhiques*, V, Brussels, 1936–1937, pp. 223–242; *Musila et Narada*, *ibid.*, pp. 189–222.
Sénart, Émile, "Bouddhisme et Yoga," in *Revue de l'Histoire des Religions*, XLII, 1900, pp. 345–363.

ON TANTRISM:

Abhinavagupta, *Tantrasara* (Italian translation by Raniero Gnoli), Turin, 1960.
Eliade, M., *Le Yoga*, etc., *op. cit.*, pp. 205–344, 385–407 discussion of Tantrist doctrines and practices, bibliography).
Snellgrave, David, *Buddhist Himalaya*, London, 1957; *The Hevajra Tantra*, 2 vols., Oxford, 1959.
Tucci, G., *Teoria e pratica del mandala*, Rome, 1949.

ON THE SPREAD OF YOGAN TECHNIQUES:

In Tibet:

Bacot, J., *Milarépa*, Paris, 1925, pp. 200 ff.; W. Y. Evans-Wentz, *Tibetan Yoga and Secret Doctrines*, Oxford, 1935 (second edition 1958); Alexandra David Neel, *Mystiques et magiciens du Tibet*, Paris, 1929, pp. 245 ff.

In Mongolia:

Pozdnezhev, A. M., "Dhyana und Samadhi im Mongolischen Lamiasmus," in *Zeitschrift für Buddhismus*, VII, 1926, pp. 378–421.

In China:

Blofeld, John, *The Path of Sudden Attainment: A Treatise of the Ch'an (Zen) School of Chinese Buddhism by Hui Hai of the T'ang Dynasty,* London, 1948.

ON PARALLEL TECHNIQUES (HOLDING THE BREATH, ETC.):

Bloom, Dr. André, "L'Hésychasme, Yoga chrétien," in *Yoga,* edited by J. Masui, Paris, 1953, pp. 177–195.

Eliade, M., *Le Yoga,* etc., *op. cit.,* pp. 71–78, 220–223, 392, 395–396.

Gardet, L., "La mention du nom divin (dhikr) dans la mystique musulmane," in *Revue thomiste,* 1952, pp. 641–679; 1953, pp. 197–213.

Gouillard, Jean, *Petite philocalie de la prière du coeur,* Paris, 1953.

Hausherr, Irénée, S. J., "La Méthode d'oraison hésychaste," in *Orientalia Christiana,* IX, 2; Rome, 1927; "L'Hésychasme: étude de spiritualité," in *Orientalia Christiana Periodica,* Rome, 1956, pp. 5–40, 247–285.

Maspéro, Henri, "Les procédés de 'nourrir le Principe vital' dans la religion taoïste," in *Journal asiatique,* 1937, pp. 171–252, 353–430.

Moreno, M., "Mistica musulmana e mistica indiana," in *Annali Lateranensi,* 1946, pp. 102–212, especially pp. 140 ff.

Nolle, W., "Hesychasmus und Yoga," in *Byzantinische Zeitschrift,* Vol. XLVII, pp. 95–103.

ON YOGA IN MODERN INDIA:

Audobindo, Sri, *The Synthesis of Yoga, Part I: The Yoga of Divine Works,* Madras, 1948. (New, revised edition including the first twelve chapters published in the magazine, *Arya,* under the same title between January and November, 1915); *La Synthèse des Yogas,* Vol. I: *Le Yoga des Oeuvres divines,* Paris, 1939 (English translation of the first six chapters in *Arya*); *Lights on Yoga,* Howrah, 1935 (extracts from letters to disciples); *Bases of Yoga,* Calcutta, 1936 (extracts from letters); *More Lights on Yoga,* Pondichery, 1948 (extracts from letters to disciples); *Elements of Yoga (New Letters With Questions),* Pondichery, 1953.

Monod-Herzen, G. E., *Shri Audobindo,* Paris, 1954 (especially pp. 61–181 and 257–275).

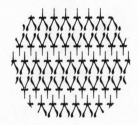

Index